WILTSHIRE
RAILWAYS

WILTSHIRE RAILWAYS

COLIN G. MAGGS

HALSGROVE

First published in Great Britain in 2009

British Library Cataloguing-in-Publication Data
A CIP record for this title is available from the British Library

ISBN 978 1 84114 911 0

HALSGROVE
Halsgrove House,
Ryelands Industrial Estate,
Bagley Road, Wellington, Somerset TA21 9PZ
Tel: 01823 653777   Fax: 01823 216796
email: sales@halsgrove.com

Part of the Halsgrove group of companies
Information on all Halsgrove titles is available at: www.halsgrove.com

Printed and bound in Great Britain by CPI Antony Rowe, Wiltshire

Contents

RAILWAYS OF WILTSHIRE

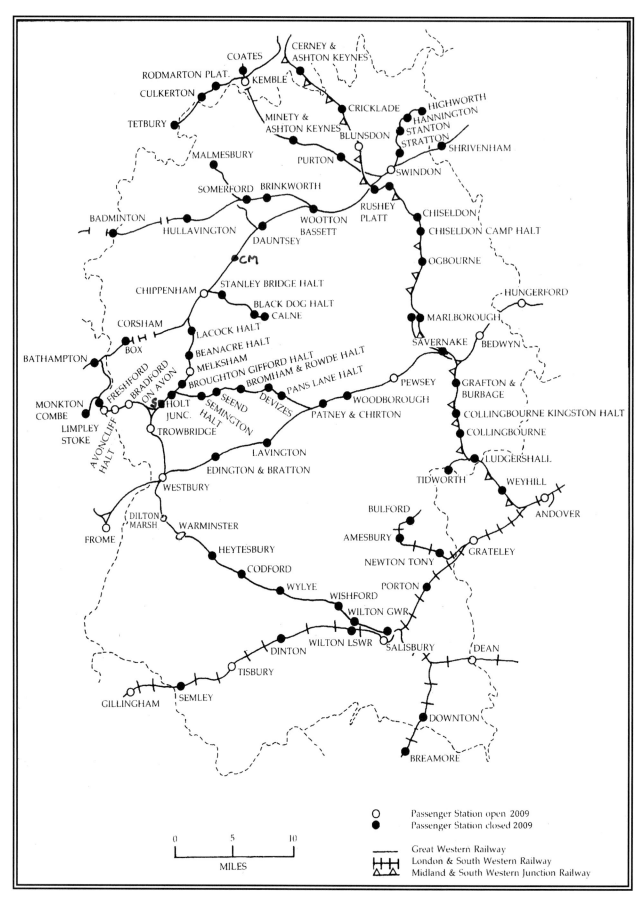

COATES
CERNEY &
ASHTON KEYNES
RODMARTON PLAT.
KEMBLE
CULKERTON
TETBURY
MINETY &
ASHTON KEYNES
CRICKLADE
HIGHWORTH
HANNINGTON
STANTON
STRATTON
SHRIVENHAM
MALMESBURY
BLUNSDON
PURTON
SWINDON
SOMERFORD
BRINKWORTH
RUSHEY
PLATT
CHISELDON
BADMINTON
HULLAVINGTON
WOOTTON
BASSETT
CHISELDON CAMP HALT
DAUNTSEY
CM
OGBOURNE
STANLEY BRIDGE HALT
CHIPPENHAM
BLACK DOG HALT
CALNE
HUNGERFORD
CORSHAM
MARLBOROUGH
LACOCK HALT
SAVERNAKE
BEDWYN
BOX
BEANACRE HALT
BATHAMPTON
MELKSHAM
BROUGHTON GIFFORD HALT
BROMHAM & ROWDE HALT
FRESHFORD
BRADFORD
ON AVON
PANS LANE HALT
PEWSEY
GRAFTON &
BURBAGE
MONKTON
COMBE
HOLT
JUNC.
SEMINGTON
HALT
SEEND
DEVIZES
WOODBOROUGH
COLLINGBOURNE KINGSTON HALT
LIMPLEY
STOKE
AVONCLIFF
HALT
TROWBRIDGE
PATNEY & CHIRTON
COLLINGBOURNE
LAVINGTON
LUDGERSHALL
EDINGTON & BRATTON
TIDWORTH
WEYHILL
WESTBURY
BULFORD
ANDOVER
DILTON
MARSH
WARMINSTER
AMESBURY
GRATELEY
FROME
HEYTESBURY
NEWTON TONY
CODFORD
PORTON
WYLYE
WISHFORD
WILTON GWR
WILTON LSWR
SALISBURY
DEAN
DINTON
TISBURY
DOWNTON
GILLINGHAM
SEMLEY
BREAMORE

○ Passenger Station open 2009
● Passenger Station closed 2009

—— Great Western Railway
      London & South Western Railway
      Midland & South Western Junction Railway

0   5   10

MILES

S: Staverton Halt
CM: Christian Malford Halt

Dedicated to the very helpful
Richard V. Forse

1 An Outline Survey of Railways in Wiltshire

When 'WILTSHIRE' and 'railway' are mentioned most people think of the Great Western Railway (GWR) and of its works at Swindon in particular. This is a very biased view and in fact the railways of Wiltshire can be divided into groups. The GWR and its associates served mainly the northern half of the county; the London & South Western Railway (LSWR) passed east to west along the southern border of Wiltshire; and the Midland & South Western Junction Railway (MSWJR) ran north to south linking the GWR and the LSWR. Finally there were a significant number of military railways and also a number of stone quarry railways in the Box and Bradford on Avon area.

The GWR and its allies, the Wilts, Somerset & Weymouth Railway (WSWR) and the Cheltenham & Great Western Union Railway (CGWUR), favoured the broad gauge of 7 ft 0 ¼ in between the rails since this gave a stable and safe ride and space for larger and more economic wagons. So stable were trains on the broad gauge that when a passenger train crashed into the rear of a goods train on Dauntsey Bank at 50 mph, only a few passengers were injured, in fact some remained asleep and only woke after the train returned to Chippenham. Quite unaware that they had travelled to Dauntsey and back, they complained at the lengthy time the train had spent at Chippenham!

Although the choice of gauge mattered little in the early days of railways when each line was an entirety in itself, as the railway network grew, differing gauges prevented through running and it was found that unity of gauge was essential. Although the broad gauge had the edge on standard gauge, there were many more miles of standard gauge track in England and Wales as a whole and it was more economic to narrow a broad gauge line than to shift platforms and other line-side structures, widen bridges, cuttings and embank-

8

ments. Sometimes a line was completely transformed to standard gauge while other broad gauge lines had a third rail added so that it could carry a train of either gauge. Usually a train was entirely of one gauge, but sometimes it contained rolling stock of two gauges. The very last broad gauge train ran on 21 May 1892. By this date the GWR had absorbed the CGWUR in 1843 and the WSWR in 1850. The LSWR and the MSWJR were both standard gauge lines with 4 ft 8½ in between the rails.

The first LSWR line in Wiltshire was the branch from Bishopstoke, now Eastleigh, to Salisbury, so a trip to London was circuitous. Ten years later a

Redundant broad gauge engines on Swindon Dump 1892, following the abolition of the broad gauge. The locomotive works are in the background and St Mark's Church, right. (Author's collection)

Midland & South Western Junction Railway 4-4-0 No 9 and a 2-4-0 stand outside Swindon Town shed 15 September 1923. (F. H. Smith)

Aerial view of Swindon Junction: The passenger station in the foreground; the GWR workers' housing estate top left; the main line to Bristol straight ahead with the carriage and wagon works to the left and the locomotive works to the right. The line to Gloucester curves to the top right. (Author's collection)

direct line was opened and extended to Exeter. The MSWJR began as the Swindon, Marlborough & Andover Railway and then when the northern extension, the Swindon and Cheltenham Extension Railway was built, the two united to become the MSWJR. In both World Wars it proved a vital link taking troops and supplies to the south coast and returned with the wounded.

Prior to the First World War Salisbury Plain was used for military training and during that war several military railways were laid to serve the camps, particularly those near Dinton, Amesbury, Tidworth and in the Wylye Valley.

Many of the branch lines were closed either immediately following, or before the 1963 Beeching Report on Railways. The only preserved line in Wiltshire is the Blunsdon to Cricklade section of the MSWJR which was re-laid and re-opened.

Wiltshire has two main railway centres: Swindon and Salisbury. Swindon was an important junction and had the GWR's main works for constructing locomotives, carriages and wagons. Salisbury was and is the junction where the Waterloo to Exeter line is crossed by that from Bristol to Southampton and Portsmouth. In the steam era most trains had their engines changed at Salisbury and in 1950 for example, no less than 57 locomotives were allocated to the shed.

H15 class 4-6-0 No 333 at Salisbury with a down train circa 1947. (Author's collection)

Stations were generally constructed in a position convenient for the railway, rather than for the public. With the development of competing bus services, to try and stop movement to the roads, railways opened 'halts' close to housing. Stations were manned and were required to have a waiting room and toilets, but halts were simple unmanned platforms with just a shelter.

2 How a Railway was Created

IN THE 19th century, businessmen and landowners wishing to improve trade, increase the value of their property and invest their cash profitably, might propose a scheme for linking two places by a railway. The way they went about such a scheme followed a general pattern which can be described once and serve to tell the story of the creation of almost any railway in Wiltshire. Several meetings would be called in the locality and provided that sufficient financial support was promised, a bill would be placed before Parliament, itself often proving an expensive process. Committees of the houses of Commons and Lords received evidence for and against the proposed line. If both houses passed the bill it became an Act of Parliament and the promoting company was then legally entitled to raise a stipulated sum of money to purchase land and build the railway between the two chosen places. Before going to Parliament a surveyor would have drawn up plans. Ideally, a line would be straight, level, and pass through or close to chief settlements, yet using cheaper, rather than expensive land. If tunnels, cuttings and embankments were required, the surveyor would endeavour to make sure that soil excavated could be used in a nearby embankment. These plans, known as Deposited Plans, were placed with the local authority and Parliament. After the passing of the Act, with at least some of the capital raised, a contractor had to be found to carry out the work; those companies with less money would seek a contractor willing to work for shares rather than for cash.

Work usually began with the ceremonial turning of the first turf, a highly decorated spade being used to lift a sod into an equally ornate wheelbarrow. This was often done by the company's chairman or his wife. After the ceremony the directors and local dignitaries dined. The contractor set to work and was likely to meet difficulties – shortage of workers or materials, hard rock in an unexpected place that had to be cut through, or fluid clay that

(Left) The new bridge over Station Road, Westbury, 30 June 1931. The Westbury cut-off was opened 1 January 1933. (Author's collection)

(Right) Construction of the Patney & Chirton to Westbury direct line circa 1898. (Author's collection)

refused to stay in place. The railway company might be unable to raise enough money to pay the contractor or the contractor himself might go bankrupt. Parliament wisely decided that a railway company must deposit a sum of money so that in the event of failure to complete the line after work had started, the money deposited could be used to re-instate the property purchased compulsorily from the landowners. The Act of Parliament stipulated that a line should be completed within a certain period of time and quite often, because of various difficulties, the railway was forced to apply to Parliament for an extension of time and not infrequently for an increase in capital to cover unforeseen costs.

When the contractor completed the line and before it could be opened to passenger traffic, an inspection had to be undertaken for the Board of Trade through an officer of the Royal Engineers. He went over the line testing bridge and other structures, making sure that the signalling was adequate for safety and the stations had suitable facilities. Usually at least one fault was discovered. If it was minor the Board of Trade granted a certificate subject to its correction; if there was major criticism, re-inspection was required before the line could be opened.

On the opening day the directors and local dignitaries travelled over the line, dining afterwards. If the railway was a local one, it was usually worked

Lord Bruce cuts the first sod of the Swindon, Marlborough & Andover Railway at Marlborough on 28 July 1875. (Author's collection)

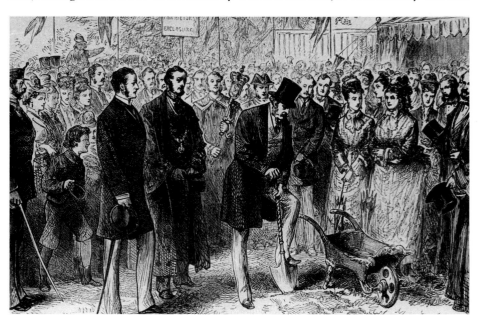

by a larger company to make the business more economic. That was because, although perhaps the line might require only one engine and two passenger coaches to work normal services, at least one more engine would be needed as a spare when the other engine was having a boiler wash-out or undergoing repair. On market days, fair days and Bank Holidays two coaches might prove insufficient. Some goods traffic required special rolling stock and it would not be sensible to invest capital in something used only occasionally. To obviate such difficulties a small company therefore usually arranged for a larger company with larger resources to work the line for a percentage of the gross receipts. Some lines were far from profitable, ordinary shareholders rarely or never receiving a dividend, and it often happened that eventually a small railway was purchased by the working company, the payment usually less than its building cost.

Calne Station.

Steam rail motor No 2 at Calne. (Author's collection)

In the early 1900s rail motors came into use. A rail motor was a passenger coach and locomotive contained on the same under frame. It was designed so that when going boiler-first the engine would be at the front, but when returning the driver could walk to what had been the rear and drive from a special control compartment, the fireman remaining at the other end. The use of a rail motor obviated the time and trouble needed to run an engine round its train at the end of every journey. When a rail motor service was introduced, unmanned halts were opened at places where traffic was insufficient to warrant a staffed station.

Rail motors were found to lack flexibility. If, on (say) a market day, the number of passengers quadrupled, a rail motor could not cope as it was only powerful enough to draw one trailer. As a railway had to have a locomotive and coaches standing by for such an eventuality, then any saving made by the rail motor was lost.

Christian Malford Halt, view up 23 May 1963. The left hand road is of flat-bottomed rail while that on the right is laid with the older bullhead type. (Author)

14XX class 0-4-2T
No 1446 propels a
push and pull train
between Calne
and Chippenham.
(R. E. Toop)

The solution was a push-pull or auto train. An engine stayed at one end of the train and on the return journey, the driver could control his engine from a special compartment at what had been the rear by means of mechanical rods or compressed air.

The year 1923 brought Grouping when, apart from very minor lines, all railway companies became part of one of the Big Four: The Great Western Railway, the London, Midland & Scottish Railway (LMS); the London & North Eastern Railway (LNER) and the Southern Railway (SR). The GWR was the only railway to retain its old name, the London & South Western Railway becoming part of the SR and the MSWJR was absorbed by the GWR. With Nationalisation on 1 January 1948 the GWR became British Railways Western Region, and the SR the Southern Region, though minor area changes were made.

Railways were quick to spot the bus competitor and themselves participated in road transport, the GWR owning its first bus in 1903, though its first service in Wiltshire, between Marlborough and Calne opened 10 October 1904. The LSWR operated several bus routes, but none within Wiltshire.

From 1928 legislation permitted railways to purchase large, but not controlling, shareholdings in existing bus companies. The GWR and SR reached agreement with the National Omnibus & Transport Company: the Western National was set up to run bus services in GWR territory, the railway agreeing to transfer its road motor services to that company in return for a half share, the Western National undertaking to co-ordinate rail and road services and not to compete with the railway. The Southern National operated similar

Driver Johnny Dawes at Calne 1930 with GWR Thornycroft bus XV 5108. (Percy Vines)

services in the SR area. From 1 January 1929 the GWR also owned shares in the Bristol Tramways & Carriage Company.

In addition to bus competition, the increase in private car ownership in the 1950s and 1960s was another reason for the decline in the number of rail passengers and many of the poorly-frequented stations closed. The smaller stations remaining open were generally unstaffed, passengers purchasing their tickets from the conductor-guard on the diesel multiple unit pay trains. Freight traffic also declined because of increased use of road vehicles, especially at times when railwaymen were on strike, their actions permanently damaging business. The swing to the use of electricity, North Sea gas and oil for heating brought a decrease in the once very heavy coal traffic to almost every station. Fifty years ago railways carried relatively small loads to a variety of destinations; today the railways are mainly bulk carriers of stone, steel, cars, coal and oil.

3 **The Great Western Railway**

IN THE AUTUMN of 1824, that is almost a year before the opening of the Stockton & Darlington Railway, a group of Bristol merchants proposed a locomotive-worked line between their city, then the second largest in the kingdom, and London.

The London & Bristol Rail-Road Company's line surveyed by John Macadam, provided a turnpike road for riders and carriages alongside the rails. Although it was stated that all the shares were taken up, no application was made for an Act of Parliament and the project died. Following the success of the Stockton & Darlington and the Liverpool & Manchester lines, the idea of a Bristol to London railway was revived in 1832, a committee appointing a young man of 27, Isambard Kingdom Brunel as engineer. He carried out the necessary survey and recommended a route through Bath, Chippenham, Swindon, the Vale of White Horse and the Thames Valley. Meanwhile London friends and business associates of the many Bristol merchants who had become interested in the project, caught their enthusiasm and formed a committee in the metropolis.

The first joint meeting of the two committees was held in London on 19 August 1833. They adopted the grand title the Great Western Railway instead of the prosaic Bristol & London Rail-Road. The GWR bill was 250 ft in length, weighed over 9 lb and was made up of 130 parchment skins, each about 23 in by 10 in. Brunel was a man of ideas and refused to adopt slavishly the gauge of 4 ft 8½ in chosen by Stephenson. As Brunel explained in a letter to his directors, the centre of gravity could be lowered by having locomotives and carriage and wagon bodies inside the wheels instead of above. It was for this reason that the broad gauge was adopted and explains why Brunel's vertical clearance was only a little higher than that of the standard gauge party.

The construction of 118½ miles of railway from London to Bristol was far too great an undertaking to be completed all at once, so it was necessarily built and opened in stages of up to 22 miles in length. The first section to be

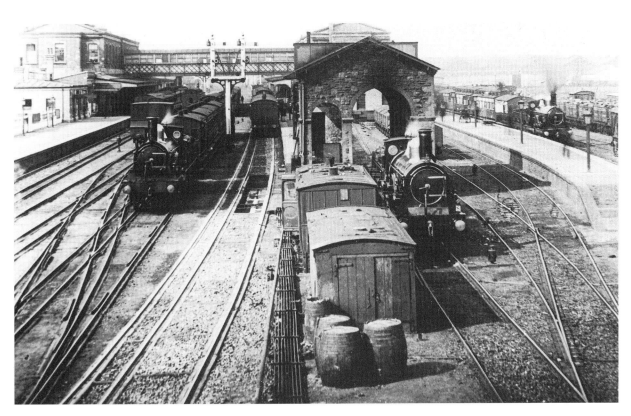

opened was from Paddington to Maidenhead in 1838 and two years later it reached Reading. From this date the Bath and Bristol stage coaches connected with the trains.

It reached Faringdon Road (later named Challow), 20 July 1840. As this station was on the main road to Cirencester, Gloucester and Cheltenham, it was in a good position for transferring traffic from rail to road or vice versa. A few months later the line was extended into Wiltshire and through Swindon to Hay Lane, or Wootton Bassett Road, on 17 December 1840. Hay Lane only had a temporary platform, but was suitable as a terminus for a short time as it was within ½ mile of a turnpike road. The GWR directors arranged for Bath coaches (the line had opened between Bristol and Bath on 31 August 1840), to work at a fixed rate carrying passengers and parcels booked by the railway and similar arrangements were made for the conveyance of goods.

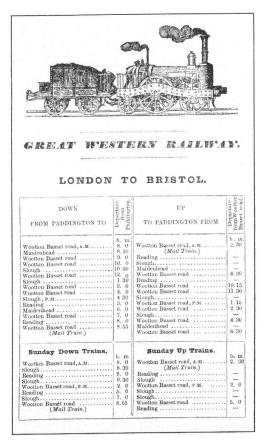

A GWR time table of 17 December 1840.

Swindon Junction view down circa 1891. Notice the mixed gauge track with its complicated pointwork, left. A small engine shed is at the up bay platform. On the far right a train has arrived from Gloucester. A grounded van and coach in the foreground are recycled as huts. (Author's collection)

Cheltenham and Gloucester traffic continued to run from Faringdon Road as the roads between Hay Lane and Cirencester were 'in such bad repair as to be almost impassable'. The railway was unable to reach Wootton Bassett as Studley cutting remained incomplete. Swindon itself was not given a station at this date.

That autumn the company's locomotive engineer, Daniel Gooch, wrote a letter to Brunel using these arguments in favour of locating the railway works at Swindon:

a) It was the junction with the Cheltenham line.

b) East of Swindon the line was virtually flat, whereas to the west were the 1 in 100 gradients of Wootton Bassett and Box and bank engines for the former incline could be shedded at Swindon.

c) The selection of Swindon would divide the line into three equal parts: to Reading; to Swindon and to Bristol.

d) The railway crossed the Wilts & Berks Canal at Swindon giving a direct connection with the Somerset coalfield. (It is interesting that locomotive coal had to travel by water.) The canal and its reservoir at Coate could supply water in an emergency.

On 25 February 1841 the GWR directors concurred with Gooch.

Swindon running shed: 43XX class 2-6-0 No 5370 left, 74XX class 0-6-0PT No 7418, 57XX class 0-6-0PT No 3776 and 55XX class 2-6-2T No 5538 right. (M. E. J. Deane)

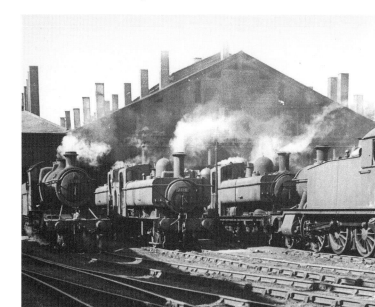

The cuttings and embankments between Hay Lane and Chippenham caused trouble through the clay slipping. In one place Brunel used the expensive and time-consuming expedient of driving lines of piles through the embankment into solid ground below and then chaining those lines of piles together. The line was extended to Chippenham on 31 May 1841.

The completion of the 3,212 yd long Box Tunnel delayed the opening through to Bath. Although its portals are stone, the tunnel is lined with brick

The west portal of Box Tunnel circa 1910. Repairs have been made and 'formers' may be seen leaning on the embankment, right. (Author's collection)

and there are reported to be a million faggots of wood placed between the top of the brick arch and the stone roof to prevent falling rock smashing the brick arches. Access doors are provided so that this space can be inspected.

The tunnel is straight and the rising sun shines through on 6 and 7 April. For some time these dates were queried, but were confirmed by BR engineers who made observations in 1988. If there was no refraction the sun would shine through on Brunel's birthday, 9 April, but Bessel's Refraction Tables were not readily available in England in the 1830s. The earth's atmosphere causes a slight bend of the sun's rays which enables us to see the sun rising three minutes before it is actually there, geometrically speaking, and likewise we see it setting three minutes after it has gone.

Ears 'pop' when entering Box Tunnel as air is slightly compressed by the train because the walls prevent it from being displaced outwards. This causes air on the outside of the ear to be slightly denser than that on the inside. Moving the jaw equalises the pressure more quickly. On leaving the tunnel ears 'pop' as the pressure slightly decreases.

The line opened through to Bath on 30 June 1841, thus completing the route to Bristol.

The opening of the GWR affected parts of Wiltshire not served by the railway. For instance, before the GWR opened, thirty to forty coaches a day ran through Marlborough, but the advent of the GWR reduced this number to five. The £2000 paid annually to horse keepers and helpers and then spent within Marlborough was no longer received. From the spring of 1840 only one Bath coach proceeded all the way by road from Bath to London without using the railway. The *Bath & Cheltenham Gazette* of 28 April 1840 recorded that innkeepers between Bath and Reading were 'starving' and that the value of tavern property within that area had been reduced within the last two to three years by 60 to 80 per cent.

The 10.30am Paddington to Plymouth passes Swindon Junction on 1 October 1895. This was the second train to pass through non-stop. (Author's collection)

The first station entering Wiltshire was Stratton Park Halt opened 20 November 1933 to serve the eastern suburbs of Swindon. Two platforms, each surmounted by a corrugated iron shelter, were built at a total cost of about £450. It was not a roaring success. 1,727 tickets were issued in the first full year and in 1935 fell to only 450. The station closed on 7 December 1964 when the Didcot to Swindon local passenger service was withdrawn.

Swindon Euro Freight terminal opened 24 March 2007 and Honda plans to send up to 2 trains weekly, each transporting 200 cars through the Channel Tunnel and on to its Euro Vehicle Logistics Operation in Ghent, Belgium.

At Highworth Junction the Highworth Branch (see page 29) joined before Swindon Junction station is reached, this opened 14 July 1842.

Brunel designed the station with two island platforms, each with a 3-storey stone building. To facilitate exchange between the Bristol and Gloucester lines, trains to and from Bristol used the inner platforms and those for Gloucester, the outer. Each of the buildings had offices and kitchens in the basement; waiting and refreshment rooms at platform level on the first floor, and hotel accommodation on the second floor. The buildings were linked by a covered footbridge used by hotel guests and passengers until a subway was constructed in 1870.

As the cost of building the GWR exceeded the estimate, its directors thought they had been smart when they signed a contract for Messrs J & C Rigby to construct the station for nothing and lease it to the GWR for a penny a year, the railway company undertaking to stop all passenger trains at Swindon for 10 minutes. The plan was that Messrs Rigby would recoup their costs from the catering profits.

Initially the bargain was fine, but with the development of railway services and the introduction of faster trains, the 10 minute wait proved frustrating. Eventually the GWR purchased the lease for £100,000 and on 1 October 1895 expresses passed through Swindon non-stop for the first time.

Swindon Junction following the fire on the up platform 26 March 1898. (Author's collection)

On 26 March 1898 the up station building caught fire. What was the cause? The chimney was Z-shaped and thus encouraged soot to be deposited. Another poor design feature was a timber beam running across the chimney and matters were not helped by a lead gas pipe running down the flue.

Following the withdrawal of local trains, traffic was concentrated on the former up island platform. A drawback to this scheme was that a down train requiring the use of a platform had to cross the up through road. To obviate this problem, Platform 4 on the down side of the station opened on 2 June 2003.

Immediately west of the station the Gloucester line curves northwards, while that to Bristol passed the locomotive shops to the north side and carriage shops to the south. In 1948 the works covered 326 acres, 77½ of which were roofed. With dieselisation and the contraction of the railway system, various departments were shut down, the works finally closing in June 1987. One of the features of Swindon was Trip Week when employees and their families were taken by train to holiday destinations of their choice. In 1939 27,000 left Swindon in 30 special trains, leaving the town virtually deserted. With the increase of car ownership, the last trip trains ran in 1960, ordinary trains then being able to cope with the numbers wishing to travel.

A Swindon 'Trip' train to Birkenhead leaves the Works at 6.00am circa 1909. (Author's collection)

1¼ miles west of Swindon Junction was Rushey Platt Junction where the MSWJR (see page 116) curved southwards to Andover, while the GWR passed below the MSWJR to Cheltenham.

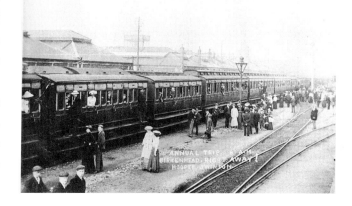

Just before Wootton Bassett station, between 1927 and 1972 a siding led to the United Dairies' creamery. The dairy used the first bulk milk tanks to run in England and this rang the death knell of the milk churn. 176 churns needed three vans and weighed a total of 80 tons, whereas the same volume of milk could be carried in a tank wagon totalling only 22 tons. The cork insulation was so effective that the milk only rose by one degree Farenheit on its journey to Willesden.

Milk tankers at Wootton Bassett creamery; they are filled beneath the archway. (Christopher Kent)

The original station at Wootton Bassett was a Brunel building in limestone, but to cope with the opening of the Bristol & South Wales Direct Railway (see page 35) it was rebuilt in 1902 in red brick. Like all stations on the line except Chippenham, it closed 4 October 1965 when stopping passenger services were withdrawn.

Dauntsey station was opened 1 February 1868 and later became the junction with the Malmesbury Railway (see page 38). An interesting feature

Wootton Bassett, view towards Swindon circa 1880; the goods shed is left and the passenger station beyond. Notice the horse shunting. (Author's collection)

Wootton Bassett view up circa 1920. Part of the bridge beyond the signal has been whitened to improve sighting. Notice that the right hand canopy covers both platform and station approach. (Author's collection)

The Brunellian building at Dauntsey, view up circa 1960. (Lens of Sutton)

The Avon Viaduct near Christian Malford 4 April 2002. (Author)

The curious pair of bridges at Langley Burrell 4 April 2002: that on the left carries road traffic and that on the right is for Maud Heath's Causeway and known as 'The Steamer'. (Author)

2201 class 2-4-0 No 2218 at Chippenham with an up stopping train circa 1905. Notice the train shed. (Author's collection)

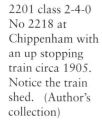

of the station was that the water tank was gravity-fed from the adjacent Wilts & Berks Canal. The canopy sheltering the bay platform for Malmesbury trains was recycled and can be seen today at Yatton on the Bristol to Weston super Mare line.

Christian Malford Halt opened 18 October 1926. As the platforms were only 150 ft in length, alighting passengers were required to travel in the last two coaches. South of the halt is the brick-built 72 yd long Avon Viaduct.

Just before Chippenham the branch from Calne (see page 43) joined. The principal buildings at Chippenham on what was the down platform, are now Grade 2 listed. The opening of the Wilts, Somerset & Weymouth Railway

required the station to be enlarged 1856-7 to cope with the increased traffic. Today the station enjoys heavy commuter traffic, in fact people on the east side of Bath prefer Chippenham to Bath. Chippenham has the works of the Westinghouse Brake & Signal Company. West of the station is the Grade 2 90 yd long Chippenham Viaduct.

At Thingley Junction the WSWR (see page 48) branches off. During the Second World War the area between Thingley Junction and the Wiltshire border west of Box, was a vast ammunition dump and at Thingley Junction were sidings for the reception and despatch of ammunition trains.

Chippenham locomotive depot circa 1908. A 2-4-0T or 0-4-2T is on the left while right is a 'Standard Goods' 0-6-0, probably No 601. On the right a locomotive coal wagon is beside the coal stage. (Edward Spearey collection)

At Thingley Junction circa 1952 54XX class 0-6-0PT No 5422 hauls an auto trailer to Chippenham from the Trowbridge direction. The main line to Bristol is on the right. (T.J. Saunders)

Corsham station viewed from Potley Bridge 23 May 1963. (Author)

H. Banks horse bus outside Corsham station circa 1900. (Author's collection)

Corsham, view up circa 1910. Blocks of stone on the wharf await transhipment by crane; also on the wharf is a 2ft 6in gauge tramway. The road roller is an Aveling & Porter product. (Author's collection)

As Corsham station was set in a cutting, each platform had merely a waiting shelter, the office building being placed at the top of the cutting. For over 20 years a pressure group has been fighting for the station to be re-opened. In the past many tons of stone left Corsham by rail. On 25 June 1935 a violent rainstorm caused the Yockney Brook to burst its bank and flood Corsham station, the line being unusable for 20 hours.

The east end of Box Tunnel has two portals: the larger for the main line and the smaller, which originally ran into an underground stone quarry which was later taken over for ammunition storage. For safety reasons, the War Department agreed not to store explosives within 100 ft of the main line tunnel.

A 4-2-2 heads an up express leaving Box Tunnel. The line into the stone quarry, right, has its sleepers covered with ballast to prevent horses tripping. (Author's collection)

Workmen at the east portal of Box Tunnel, probably July 1900 when it was closed for repairs to the inner arch. (Author's collection)

A tunnel clearance testing van in Pictor's Siding, Box, circa 1923. The crane is fitted with a cradle so that the high roof may be inspected. (Rev. W. Awdry)

4-6-0 No 7025
Sudeley Castle
passes Box (Mill
Lane) Halt with the
down Bristolian 2
April 1955. The
platforms are
immediately to the
train's rear. (R. E.
Toop)

Box, view up in
mixed gauge days.
The broad gauge
0-6-0ST is fitted
with wide buffers
enabling wagons of
either gauge to be
coupled. (Author's
collection)

Beyond Box Tunnel's west portal was Box (Mill Lane) Halt opened 31 March 1930 and set much closer to the centre of the village than was Box station. A mile to the west Farleigh Down Siding served a stone quarry. In 1939 it was used for ammunition storage. Initially it was linked by an aerial ropeway but later a 2,200 yd long narrow gauge railway in a tunnel served the storage area. Beyond the siding the GWR entered Somerset.

Box, view up circa
1910. The shed for
the banking engine
is on the far left
and cranes for
loading stone are in
the centre
background.
(Author's
collection)

4 **Branches from the Stratton Park to Box Line**

The Highworth Branch

The Swindon & Highworth Light Railway Company's Act was passed on 21 June 1875. Shares were taken up slowly, so the directors offered the unusual incentive of two shillings and sixpence to anyone able to sell a £10 share. By February 1878 £12,000 of the £21,000 required had been subscribed. A further year passed before the company was able to find a contractor willing to take £8,500 worth of shares in part payment.

14XX class 0-4-2T No 5800 working the Highworth branch goods calls at Stratton circa 1958. The passenger platform seems generously wide. (T. J. Saunders)

South Marston
platform used by
Vickers-Armstrong
workers. The
sidings are rather
overgrown. (T. J.
Saunders)

14XX class 0-4-2-T
No 5800
approaches Stanton
circa 1958. The
station building is
of timber. (T. J.
Saunders)

No 5800 at
Hannington,
apparently passing
through a meadow.
(T. J. Saunders)

No 5800 approaches Highworth station. Notice the check rail to prevent the left hand wheels bearing too heavily on the right rail. (T. J. Saunders)

1366 class 0-6-0PT No 1366 at Highworth. The coach set is branded 'Highworth' on the end panel. (Author's collection)

14XX class 0-4-2T No 5804 at Highworth. (Author's collection)

The ceremony of cutting the first turf took place at Highworth on 6 March 1879 the North Wilts Herald reporting:

> A small area had been roped off for the Ceremony and near this the Directors, Shareholders, etc., had been placed in a special area with the Ladies. Such was the attendance that this place quickly became full with results which can best be described as hilarious; the ropes gave way and the Dignitaries, Ladies and others fell into an undignified heap. The band, under Bandmaster Hawkins, continued to play unconcernedly.

The Board of Trade inspection revealed deficiencies: facing points were not interlocked; level crossing gates were unlit; the ballast was of insufficient depth and no turntable was provided at Highworth. As the company was already in debt, no funds were available to carry out these requirements so the only option was to sell to the GWR. The GWR absorbed the company in August 1882 and carried out the necessary improvements, though no turntable was installed as the line was to be worked by tank engines. The ceremonial first train ran on 8 May 1883 the 14 vehicles being hauled by two engines. The line opened to the public on the following day.

The branch was one of the last on the GWR to be worked by four-wheeled passenger coaches. They were retained as the branch loading gauge was a foot less than the GWR's standard restriction. The problem was solved eventually by the simple expedient of placing the ventilators well down the roof side instead of near the top. Following the withdrawal of passenger services on 2 March 1953, goods and workmen's trains continued to run. An unusual feature of the latter was that they were hauled by a Class 03 diesel-mechanical locomotive, normally used for short-haul goods trains or shunting, and rarely seen drawing passenger coaches. The Swindon end of the truncated branch is still used for freight.

The Cheltenham & Great Western Union Railway

Directly the GWR bill had been passed by Parliament, some enterprising folk of Cheltenham produced a scheme for linking their town with the new railway at Swindon. It received its Act on 21 June 1836, but as people were slow in subscribing, it was wisely decided that the company should concentrate on the section between Swindon and Cirencester and from that railhead coaches would be run to Stroud, Gloucester and Cheltenham. The opening, expected to be in January 1841 was delayed by an embankment slipping at Purton. This embankment was about 1¾ miles long and 20 ft high. It was formed of clay excavated from side cuttings and became sodden in the wet winter of 1839-40. Several slips occurred the following year and it was found that the core of the bank was saturated and very soft. At one spot it forced in the side of a cottage. To cure the trouble, Brunel burnt clay on the slopes and filled in the side cuttings where the bank had collapsed.

The CGWUR opened to Cirencester on 31 May 1841 and the town, instead of being merely at the end of a branch off the Cheltenham line, found itself temporarily the main station. The CGWUR was taken over by the GWR on 10 May 1844 and for only £230,000 acquired a partly completed line on which £600,000 had been spent and which had the potential of becoming an important through line. It is interesting to note that the GWR timetables stated that London time was about 7½ minutes before Cirencester time. It was, of course, the ease and speed of travel which railways brought about, which led to the adoption of Greenwich Mean Time in England. To complete the story, the line opened to Gloucester 12 May 1845 and conversion to standard gauge took place on 25 and 26 May 1872. Until the opening of the Severn Tunnel in 1886, trains to and from South Wales travelled via Gloucester and used the CGWUR.

Bremell Sidings 13 June 1986, view east from a DMU. The main line was singled 28 July 1968. (Author)

North of Swindon Junction the line crossed the MSWJR and beyond were Bremell Sidings opened 7 November 1943 for oil storage. Purton station had its original timber station building on the up platform replaced about 1960

Purton view down in the early nineteen-thirties. (D. Thompson)

(Top) Minety &
Ashton Keynes
view down 31 May
1962. (Author)

(Right) A down
broad gauge train
approaches Purton
in an early view of
one of Brunel's less
grand stations.
(Author's
collection)

Oaksey Halt, view
up circa 1963.
(Lens of Sutton)

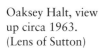

by a flat-roofed brick building which still sur-
vives as 'Station Garage'. The station closed
to passengers 2 November 1964 as did the
other stations on this line in Wiltshire.

Minety & Ashton Keynes was a typical
Brunelian chalet-style station in brick with
stone dressings. Oaksey Halt opened on 18
February 1929 and dealt with milk as well as
passengers. Beyond the line passes into
Gloucestershire.

The Bristol & South Wales Direct Railway

During the latter half of the nineteenth century people often jokingly said that the initials 'GWR' stood for Great Way Round' and certainly many of the Great Western's main lines were far from being direct.

When the Severn Tunnel was first used by passenger trains in 1886, expresses from London to South Wales had to curve southwards at Wootton Bassett, pass through Bath and Bristol and then bear northwards again to reach the tunnel. Trains were obviously travelling an unnecessary mileage and a direct link was needed through the southern end of the Cotswolds between Wootton Bassett and Filton, north of Bristol.

James C Inglis, chief engineer of the GWR, piloted the bill with such skill that no opposition was encountered in the Parliamentary Committee stage. The estimated cost of the 33½ miles of line was £1,300,000. The Act was passed on 7 August 1896 and the contract for construction let to S. Pearson & Son early the following year.

The undertaking was the biggest of the kind to be carried out since the extension of the Great Central Railway to London a few years before. The contractor's plant consisted of 75 miles of temporary lines; 50 locomotives; 17 steam navvies; 11 steam cranes; 1,800 earth wagons and three large brickworks specially built. More than 4,000 men were employed. 50 million bricks and 20,000 tons of cement and lime were used.

The line was laid for speedy running, no gradient being steeper than 1 in 300 and no curve sharper than one mile radius. Considering that the line had to cross the Cotswold Hills, this was a fine achievement. Four of the stations had quadruple track enabling non-stop trains to by-pass the platforms, and, if necessary, overtake slower ones. Most of the embankments were wide enough to allow for quadrupling throughout and the length of the two tunnels totalled nearly three miles; the three viaducts had a total of 28 arches, while in addition were 88 bridges.

The first section of the line to be opened was from Wootton Bassett to Badminton on 1 January 1903, but only for goods traffic. The first through goods train to use the whole of the line left Bristol at 8.30 am on 1 May 1903. The first passenger train, the 6.32 am used the line two months later on 1 July. It carried the Superintendent of the Bristol Division of the GWR and several company officials, but there was no special opening ceremony, though children at most schools along the line were given a holiday. Four new direct expresses from Paddington to South Wales were run over the line.

The BSWDR may well have been used to break a speed record. In May 1906, No 2903 *Lady of Lyons* proved that a newly-built locomotive could achieve 100 mph without causing mechanical harm. It was the practice to send new engines on trial trips from Swindon to Stoke Gifford and back. No 2903 was held at Chipping Sodbury until the line was clear to Wootton Bassett. At last the signal fell and the driver gave the engine her head. The timing for some distance by the quarter mileposts was given as 120 mph, while the clocking between the signal boxes of Little Somerford and Hullavington was booked as two minutes for the four and a half miles. This works out as 135 mph, probably a rather generous result, but certainly the speed must have been in excess of 120 mph, thus antedating the exploits of today's High Speed Trains by 70 years and perhaps *Lady of Lyons* may have reached a speed higher than the 126 mph of *Mallard*.

28XX class 2-8-0 No 2861 passes through Brinkworth with an up goods 15 June 1962. (Author)

Brinkworth was the first station after leaving Wootton Bassett. It was of the standard GWR design for a small country station on the line, having a brick construction with slated roof and window sills and heads, and chimney caps in Forest of Dean bluestone. Only the centre stretch of the platforms was paved, the outer sections consisting of stone chippings. In addition to the station master's house, three cottages were constructed for signalmen. Traffic was light, only four trains stopped daily at each platform. The station closed entirely 3 April 1961, the date when passenger services were withdrawn from all other stations on this line in Wiltshire.

The four road Little Somerford station view up circa 1910. Notice the foot grips on the platform ramp. (Author's collection)

The Bristol &
South Wales Direct
Railway crosses the
erstwhile
Malmesbury
branch, though at
the date taken, 23
August 1955, this
length of the
branch had been
reduced to a siding.
(Author)

During The First
World War, soldiers
guard an over bridge
at Little Somerford
from demolition by
German activists.
(Author's collection)

Little Somerford station had four tracks: two platform roads for stopping passenger trains or goods trains waiting to be overtaken, and two through lines. From 1933 Little Somerford became the junction station for the Malmesbury Branch (see page 38). West of the station the line crossed the Malmesbury Branch via the 150 yd long Somerford Viaduct.

Hullavington was a double track station similar to that at Brinkworth. Initially a pair of cottages was built for the signalmen, but when a third was

Hullavington, view up circa 1905. Notice that the up platform is of timber. (Author's collection)

appointed in the mid-thirties, an additional house was built. Beyond the station the line passes into Gloucestershire.

The Malmesbury Railway

The Malmesbury Railway was unique in that it changed its junction from one main line to another of equal importance.

The Malmesbury Railway seal: this company was taken over by the GWR on 1 July 1892. (Author's collection)

Although mentioned in a railway scheme as early as 1864, this project foundered, but eventually the Malmesbury Railway Act was passed on 25 July 1872, the line making a junction with the GWR at Dauntsey, the BSWDR being very much in the future. The success of the Malmesbury Railway seemed assured as the GWR agreed to subscribe half of the estimated cost of £60,000 and work the line on completion. Messrs Budd & Holt were the contractors, the first sod cut on 8 July 1874.

Eventually the line was completed and on 17 December 1877 it was opened 'amid much rejoicings'. Free tickets were issued to shareholders who travelled by special train to Malmesbury and were received by a procession of leading inhabitants.

Regular traffic started the next day and a mishap occurred, the *Swindon Advertiser* of 22 December reporting:

> Accident on the Malmesbury and Dauntsey Railway – An accident happened on Tuesday on the new line of railway, that was opened on the previous day from Malmesbury to Dauntsey station, but happily did not result in any material damage to life or property. The accident in

question took place at the level crossing between Dauntsey and Somerford Magna, where there was a pair of massive gates erected across the railway, and also a gate-keeper's house. As the early train was proceeding from Dauntsey, the gate-keeper failed to open the gates, and the train dashed through, shivering the gate to atoms. Beyond slight damage to the engine, no further damage was done. From inquiries it appears that the old man at the gates could not get out of the house in time owing to the handle of the door coming off in his hand. He has been in the service of the company 35 years, and this is the first accident he has ever had. There will be an inquiry into the matter.

Coffee Pot the contractor's engine and wagon used when building the Malmesbury branch. (Author's collection)

Just over two years later a tragedy was averted. As a consequence of heavy rain during the morning of 3 March 1880, Swallett's Brook rose rapidly, the strong current washing away one foundation of a pier of Poole's Bridge between Dauntsey and Somerford.

The 11.35 am from Dauntsey safely crossed the bridge, but shortly afterwards the buttress on the left bank collapsed shifting the 53 ft span by several feet. Fortunately two 16-year old boys foresaw the danger to the train returning as the 12 o'clock from Malmesbury. The *Bath & Cheltenham Chronicle* recorded that:

They ran with all speed and by extended arms and the waving of their hands succeeded in attracting the attention of the policeman at the crossing and he stopped the train which had just appeared in sight. The train proceeded slowly on until it met the lads and they informed the driver of the state of the bridge. The train was backed to Somerford where the passengers, numbering less than a dozen, got out and proceeded to walk to Dauntsey, a distance of about three miles.

For the rest of the day the Great Western provided a horse-drawn conveyance between Dauntsey and Somerford. The following day a crane lifted the bridge which was fixed temporarily so that passengers could detrain on one side, walk across and entrain on the other side. The bridge was re-opened for rail traffic on 9 March.

The Malmesbury Railway was taken over by the GWR from 1 July 1892. When the BSWDR was under construction, a temporary connection was laid from the Malmesbury branch westwards for the purpose of bringing materials to the new line. Some thirty years later, as an economy measure it was decided that a permanent connecting line should be laid alongside the up Badminton line from Little Somerford station on the new main line, to the Malmesbury branch at Kingsmead Crossing. These alterations were

The former bay platform at Dauntsey used by trains for Malmesbury until 17 July 1933. The branch curved to the right of the signal box. This view was taken 23 August 1955. (Author)

Great Somerford Halt, July 1932. The track is of flat-bottomed rail. (Author's collection)

completed by 6 February 1933 so that the branch could be worked from Little Somerford instead of Dauntsey, but a legal hitch prevented the abandonment from Kingsmead Crossing to Dauntsey. The new spur was not used until 17 July when the line between Dauntsey and Kingsmead Crossing was closed. The length of the branch was now 3¾ instead of 6½ miles.

Leaving the main line at Dauntsey the line crossed the Avon twice before reaching Great Somerford. The station building and platform were of timber construction and sold for £10 when that section of the branch was closed. A single storey cottage was built for the crossing keeper who controlled the level crossing immediately south of the station. It paralleled an overbridge with a headroom of only 7 ft. Clearly this was insufficient for many vehicles so a level crossing was provided too.

The heavy milk traffic which developed – sometimes as many as 100 cart loads of churns came from farms daily – made it necessary for a station master to be appointed. He had a large family and needed a bigger house, so this was arranged by the simple expedient of adding an upper storey in 1893 at a cost of £127. With the opening of the main line station at Little Somerford, traffic fell and Great Somerford became a halt, milk consignment notes being collected by the gate keeper, while tickets were issued and collected by the guard.

The rails between Dauntsey and Great Somerford were lifted soon after the branch was curtailed, but a short spur between Great Somerford and Kingsmead Crossing remained for stabling wagons awaiting repair. When it was being lifted in March 1959, wagons sent to pick up the old rails ran off the end of the line and knocked a hole in the former station house. North of Great Somerford the line passed under the BSWDR and came to Kingsmead Crossing where the new branch from Little Somerford joined Kingsmead Siding.

14XX class 0-4-2T No 5802 north of Kingsmead Crossing 23 August 1955. (Author)

Malmesbury 1922:
The gas tank
wagon for
replenishing
coaches' lighting
supplies has the
label 'Malmesbury'.
The track is flat-
bottomed.
(Author's
collection)

View from
Malmesbury
Tunnel towards the
station, 23 August
1955. (Author)

Just before entering Malmesbury station the branch ran through a 105 yd
long tunnel. The situation of the station was rather unusual in that it lay
beyond the town, rather than short of it as was the case with so many
branches. Possibly this was the result of the abortive Wiltshire & Gloucestershire Railway project taking the line on to Nailsworth.

Malmesbury station had attractive stone buildings, a single platform and
an engine shed. Short of the station were goods sidings, goods shed and cattle
loading dock. Goods traffic consisted mainly of coal, agricultural machinery
and general merchandise.

Several of the seven or so daily trains each way were 'mixed' – that is they
consisted of passenger coaches and goods wagons.

14XX class 0-4-2T
No 5802 at
Malmesbury 18
August 1957. This
would have been a
special as regular
passenger services
were withdrawn on
10 September 1951.
(T. J. Saunders)

On Sunday 2 October 1927 an experimental Sentinel geared locomotive was tried over the branch with a view to reducing the operating costs. The engine made a satisfactory run with a passenger train reaching a maximum speed of 38 mph, but a 'mixed' train of normal formation proved to be beyond the capacity of the loco-motive. The engine had a patent geared chain drive, steam being produced in a vertical, instead of horizontal boiler. Its appearance was curious, as everything, in-cluding the boiler, was within the large cab, only the coal bunker being outside.

13 coach trains were the longest that could be dealt with at Malmesbury, Sunday School specials being often of this length. One evening in June 1940, a 13 coach train full of evacuees arrived at Malmesbury behind two tender engines. A marquee had been set up in the station forecourt and here food was issued to the evacuees before they were marched to Malmesbury Grammar School for a medical inspection before being taken to their billets.

Sentinel vertical boiler locomotive, ex-GWR No 12 which was tried on the Malmesbury branch. (Author)

After the war, with increasing competition from road transport, passenger services were no longer economic and the last passenger train ran on 8 September 1951. The line was finally closed on 12 November 1962, the track being lifted the following year.

The Calne Branch

Until shortly before closure it was one of the very few very profitable branches in the area. It carried substantial traffic to and from the largest bacon factory in England, and apart from workers and local inhabitants, many RAF men going to and from large camps in the area.

Calne, sited on the main Bath to London road was an important staging point in coaching days, but with the opening of the GWR this ceased and

Calne became a backwater. A railway to the town would help develop trade as 16 mills and a large bacon factory were nearby.

The Act was passed on 15 May 1860, it stipulating that a £50 per day penalty would be incurred if the Wilts & Berks Canal was obstructed. The first sod was turned in a field at Studley on 25 June 1861 and contractor Richard Hattersley started work. Two years later it was revealed that expenses had been underestimated by £10,000 and that the permanent way had been poorly constructed. Matters were corrected and the Board of Trade inspector passed the line.

57XX class 0-6-0PT No 4697 has its tanks topped up at Chippenham after working the 18.37 Calne to Chippenham following the failure of a DMU 4 September 1964. (Christopher Kent)

View from a DMU from Calne approaching Chippenham 19 August 1964. (Author's collection)

It opened on the broad gauge for goods traffic on 29 October 1863, the first train arriving with about 100 pigs and other goods. The passenger opening on 3 November was declared a holiday and shops closed. The band of the 4th Wiltshire Volunteer Corps paraded through the principal streets to the station where they entered the inaugural train, an excursion to Bath. About 800 boarded, but many others were unable to get on due to it being full. Messrs Harris, who owned the bacon factory, paid their employees' fares.

During its first month the line carried 3,918 passengers, 1,781 head of livestock (chiefly pigs) and 788¼ tons of goods. Unfortunately the company's debts were so great that the only solution was to sell to the GWR which was done on 1 July 1892. The line had been converted to standard gauge between 14 and 17 August 1874.

The Great Blizzard of 1881 caused train services to be cancelled on 18 January, running not being resumed until a goods train made its way through on the afternoon of the 20th. Ten years later on 10 March 1891 in another Great Blizzard, six empty wagons of the midday goods from Calne were derailed by snow near Stanley Bridge and narrowly missed falling into the Wilts & Berks Canal. A breakdown gang from Swindon arrived that afternoon, but the line could not be cleared until the early hours of the following morning.

Around 1900 it was proposed to extend the Calne branch to Marlborough and link it with the MSWJR's Swindon to Andover line. With the development of road transport, the idea was modified to the far cheaper option of a railway bus service. Starting on 10 October 1904 it was one of the earliest motor bus services in Wiltshire and in England. Three trips were run each way daily taking 1 hr 25 min each way for the distance of 12¾ miles. The Milnes-Daimler bus seated 10 passengers inside plus two outside beside the driver, while between the driver's back and the passenger saloon was a compartment for luggage, mail, or goods. Alternatively, by sitting on flap seats, it could be used by up to eight passengers wishing to smoke.

Although the Calne branch was only 5½ miles in length it was worked by locomotives from no less than four depots: Bath, Bristol, Chippenham and Westbury.

There were two intermediate halts between Chippenham and Calne. Stanley Bridge opened on 3 April 1905 following the inauguration in February that year of a steam rail motor service. Beyond the corrugated iron pagoda passenger shelter was a timber-built milk hut known as 'the shed with the hole

A 14XX class 0-4-2T crosses Black Bridge. (Christopher Kent)

A 14XX class
0-4-2T propels
an auto coach at
Stanley Bridge Halt
circa 1951. Behind
the engine are four
vans containing
products of Messrs
Harris. (M. E. J.
Deane)

at the back'. Strangers were intrigued as to the purpose of the small gap through which the churns were inserted. Behind the halt was a space for milk carts to queue up waiting to unload. Milk traffic was so heavy that it took a quarter of an hour to load all the churns into a train.

A 14XX class
0-4-2T enters
Stanley Bridge Halt
propelling an auto
trailer and hauling
several vans.
(Author's
collection)

Black Dog Halt opened in 1873 as a private station and siding to serve the Marquis of Lansdowne's Bowood Estate, its cost of £300 being returned to the Marquis by a rebate of 20 per cent on his carriage account. At a personal cost of £598 3s 10d he provided a rent free house for the stationmaster, additionally paying part of his wages and providing four hundredweight of coal annually.

Although the Marquis permitted other passengers to use his station – fares were charged as if to or from Calne – it did not appear in the public time tables until 15 September 1952. The station was very genteel: a notice beside the office telegraph advised: 'Don't say "Hello", say "This is Black Dog Siding speaking" '. Estate traffic consisted of about 20 wagons of coal yearly inwards, outgoing traffic mainly pit props and horses going to and from stud. In addition other traders used the siding: inwards grain and outwards timber.

Calne had sidings which accommodated 178 wagons, while a feature of parcels traffic at the passenger station were Messrs Harris' branded vans with enamel labels such as 'To work between Calne and Newcastle'. Messrs Harris' traffic to local stations travelled in the luggage compartment of ordinary passenger trains. Despatch was very efficient: sausages made after 7.30 am being delivered to shops in Bath soon after 10.00 am.

Messrs Harris required a large, reliable water supply. In the early thirties a well was sunk at Langley Burrell, north east of Chippenham, and a pipeline laid across pastures, under the GWR Chippenham to Swindon line to reach the Calne branch on the Chippenham side of Black Bridge, the pipe following the railway to Calne. The water was corrosive and if a ganger walking the length observed a leak, he notified Messrs Harris. As repair work was close to

A 54XX class 0-6-0PT propels a Calne to Chippenham train into Black Dog Halt. (Author's collection)

45XX class 2-6-2T No 5566 at Calne circa 1951. The first coach is an ex-LMS vehicle. (M. E. J. Deane)

Calne, view
towards the buffers.
The vans would be
principally for
Messrs Harris'
traffic. (Author's
collection)

the running line, a lookout had to be provided for which the GWR charged
about £1 per day.

A good relationship existed between the firm and railway, Messrs Harris
giving Calne and Chippenham station and permanent way staff a large pork
pie and 1 lb sausages each Christmas.

The largest engineering feature on the branch was Black Bridge over the
Avon. Originally of timber with eight spans of 22 ft 6 in, it was replaced by
a steel structure in 1920 with two spans of 101 ft 8 in and 71 ft 2 in
respectively.

The Wilts, Somerset & Weymouth Railway

In 1844 the broad gauge Wilts & Somerset Railway was proposed to run from
Thingley Junction to Salisbury. A few months later the GWR felt it should be
extended to Weymouth in order to cut off the advance of its rival the LSWR,
so 'Weymouth' was added to the title.' In addition branches were to reach
Devizes and Radstock. The Board of Trade forced the WSWR to build a
branch from Bradford on Avon to Bath. The company was reluctant to do so,
but in the event this line carried more traffic than that to Thingley. This
section of the line proved particularly difficult to build since there were two
aqueducts carrying the Kennet & Avon Canal over the Avon and
these required adaptation so that the railway could also run under them. It
proved a tricky operation as traffic on the canal was not allowed to be
interrupted. At Avoncliff the canal banks were found to be insecure.
Interruption of canal traffic cost the GWR £100 a day – to give some idea of
this price, an agricultural labourer was paid about 10 to fifteen shillings a
week.

Although it received its Act on 30 June 1845, due to the slump following the Railway Mania, investment was slow and furthermore problems were experienced by speculators who had paid the first deposit on shares and then were unable to meet further calls. Thingley Junction to Westbury opened on 5 September 1848 and the line was extended out of Wiltshire to Frome 7 October 1850. Although the station at Bradford on Avon was finished, rails were not laid and it remained in this condition for more than seven years. The townsfolk of Bradford were furious at this state of affairs and when the WSWR was taken over by the GWR in 1850, lawsuits were issued against the company to force it to complete the line, but these failed. To complete the story, Weymouth was eventually reached on 20 January 1857, Bradford Junction to Bathampton opened on 2 February 1857 and Holt Junction to Devizes 1 July 1857. Bradfordonians were partly compensated when the line was opened as a free special ran from the town to Weymouth – though it was not the best time of the year to visit that watering place! The *Bath & Cheltenham Gazette* reported that passengers were able 'to assure their friends at Weymouth that they were no longer doomed to that perpetual state of banishment which stage coach travelling, with all its incidents of guard, driver and hotel bills had hitherto subjected them to'.

The gauge was narrowed in June 1874. 550 men worked 18 hours daily. 'Skilly', a free drink provided to give stamina, was made by boiling 1 lb oatmeal and ½ lb sugar. The men were paid 3s 3d a day plus 1s 3d food allowance and 5d an hour overtime. Shelters were erected where sleeping accommodation was scanty. Work began on 21 June 1874 and finished 25 June 1874. The line was doubled in 1885, the original earthworks having allowed for this. Thingley to Bradford Junctions was singled in 1967 as most of the potato and tomato trains from Weymouth had ceased to use that route.

At Thingley Junction on 29 August 1943 rails were laid to form a westward curve to expedite the route of ammunition trains and additionally would have proved useful in the event of bomb damage causing trains to be diverted. It was taken out of use 20 February 1955.

Lacock Halt opened on 16 October 1905 and then on 15 February 1943 Air Ministry sidings were opened together with an outermost siding for Royal Naval use. 600 tons of coal arrived weekly for the boilers of the underground works and storage areas. In the event the Air Ministry used the sidings very little and it was primarily the Admiralty which used them until closure in September 1964. Lacock closed to passengers 18 April 1966 the same day as services to Melksham, Holt and Staverton were withdrawn. During the war a dummy RAF station was established at Lacock with damaged planes. Lights

GREAT WESTERN RAILWAY.

The Alteration of the Gauge
BETWEEN
CHIPPENHAM, WEYMOUTH, SALISBURY, BATH, *and on the* EAST SOMERSET AND BRIDPORT BRANCHES, *will be completed on the*
NIGHT of the 24th INSTANT.

The Ordinary Service of Passenger Trains will be resumed on
THURSDAY, the 25th of JUNE.

J. GRIERSON,
Paddington, June, 1874.   Genl. Manager

GWR notice concerning the gauge conversion.

Lacock Halt, view up 17 March 1963. Notice the Admiralty and Air Ministry sidings, left. (Author's collection)

A 4-6-0 heads a down goods at Melksham. (Author's collection)

on the dummy runway diverted enemy planes from neighbouring real airfields. Due to the risk of bombing, people in the locality were issued with Anderson shelters.

Beanacre Halt opened 29 October 1905 and closed to passengers 7 February 1955. Between 8 January 1939 and 15 March 1948 was a War Department siding the foundations of which were on stone brought from the ammunition siding in Box Tunnel beside the main line tunnel. Lighting in the yard at Beanacre was exempted and when a preliminary air raid warning was received, an operator switched to blue lighting, though for safety, many switched it off completely. Also when a warning sounded, an engine in Beanacre yard spread the wagons out leaving a space between each one as they were loaded with explosives. Platforms were sited in the yard and road coaches conveyed workmen to an underground shadow factory.

Melksham had a pleasant stone building but this was destroyed after closure and a 'bus stop' type halt opened on 13 May 1985. Melksham station sometimes became flooded. On 31 December 1900 the 5.50am from Swindon was brought to a halt by floods and as it was impossible for assistance to be obtained from the front, the fireman swam back through the water with a 'wrong line' order. This allowed a goods engine with 20 wagons in front to be pushed back to the rear of the passenger train which was then coupled and drawn out of the water.

DMU set B433 working the 07.32 Warminster to Gloucester is the first train to call at Melksham station when it was re-opened on 13 May 1985. (Author)

Sidings to a rubber works were immediately north of the station and a flour mill siding to the south.

Broughton Gifford Halt opened 29 October 1905. Like that at Beanacre it had a low platform. Steps on an auto trailer had to be unlocked with a carriage key and then a lever moved to lower them. If a guard forget to return them to the running position, they fouled the platform of the next station.

A busy scene at Holt Junction 1905. (Author's collection)

Holt Junction view north circa 1904. The 4-4-0 with brightly burnished buffers, heads a passenger train. (Author's collection)

Holt Junction was an unusual design for the GWR as it was simply just an island platform which meant that it had no direct road access. Beavan's tannery at Holt dealt with smelly articles: inwards came skins, barrels of 'foul' oil, dyes and trucks of dog faeces for softening leather. Staverton Halt opened 16 October 1905. On 2 June 1966 the Royal train was stabled overnight at Holt Junction on the Devizes line. Staverton had a siding serving Nestle's creamery. It opened 10 September 1934 and tank wagons were conveyed to Westbury to be coupled to

The 4.15pm
Chippenham to
Westbury, DMU W
51136/49, leaves
Staverton Halt 4
August 1959.
(Author)

the London milk train. The siding closed 31 December 1966. Coal and sugar
were inwards traffic while outwards were condensed milk, milk powder and
other dairy produce.

On 10 March 1895 a loop line was opened at Bradford Junction making
a third side to the triangle and offering a through run from Bradford on Avon
to Melksham. Following singling on 26 February 1967, it closed completely
in March 1990.

View from a DMU
as it approaches
Bradford Junction
from Melksham, 13
June 1988. The
line on the right
closed in March
1990. (Author)

The line passed below Ladydown Aqueduct and arrived at Trowbridge
where the original passenger station was designed by J.Geddes, one of Brunel's
assistants. Unfortunately this building was demolished in 1984 as it was
declared unsafe. Portable buildings served until a more traditional-style block
in brick was built in 1988. In 1899 Wiltshire County Council fixed its
headquarters at Trowbridge as being easily accessible by rail from all chief

General view of the extensive Trowbridge station circa 1910. (Author's collection)

Steam rail motor No 63 at Trowbridge. The conductor-guard wears a ticket punch. (M. J. Tozer collection)

Tombstone of William Dashford in the churchyard of Holy Trinity, Trowbridge. He served the GWR for 56 years. (Author)

A new building being erected on the up platform at Trowbridge, 13 June 1988. (Author)

A 28XX class 2-8-0 at Westbury with an up empty coaching stock train. On the far right is a water crane and 'devil' lit in cold weather to prevent freezing. In the background is Westbury Iron Works. (Author's collection)

towns in the county and also with good links to Bath and Bristol. Trowbridge engine shed closed 2 June 1923 saving £283 annually. Jim Purnell, who worked at Trowbridge station about a century ago, claimed to have had the loudest voice in Great Britain. When shouting instructions he could be heard two miles away. He also called to his wife, more than a mile from the station, 'I'm knocking off now, put the kettle on'.

Westbury station, also designed by Geddes, had a train shed until 1900. With the imminent opening of the Stert cut-off, in 1899 the old station was replaced by two 600 ft long platforms. Between 1870 and 1941 a siding served Westbury Iron Works. The works itself stopped producing iron in 1908

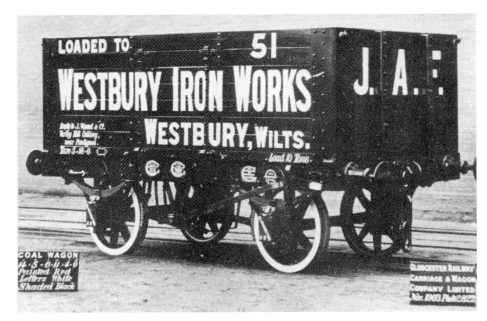

A Westbury Iron Works wagon built by the Gloucester Railway Carriage & Wagon Company in November 1903. Its livery is red. (Author's collection)

The interior of Westbury shed 12 August 1964: No 4993 *Dalton Hall* and No 6874 *Haughton Grange*. Notice the roof ducting to remove at least some of the smoke. (Revd Alan Newman)

Britannia Class 4-6-2 No 70019 *Lightning* approaches Westbury with a down express 2 July 1955. The line to Trowbridge is on the left. (R. E. Toop)

Westbury circa 1910 with the iron works beyond while a 0-4-2T stands on the right. (Author's collection)

Westbury shed yard 29 March 1965: BR Standard Class 5 4-6-0 No 73018, Hymek diesel-hydraulic D7014 and 4-6-0 No 6874 *Haughton Grange* (Revd Alan Newman)

and ore extraction ceased in 1923, but the engineering company continued to occupy the site. Due to the position of Westbury, in the weeks before D-Day, the workforce at Westbury and the number of locomotives there doubled. All the usual lodgings were full and many slept in a train of seven sleepers and two restaurant cars stabled for them specially. A 'Bulldog' class 4-4-0 supplied steam and hot water, a newly-fledged fireman throwing on a few shovelfulls of coal every hour. In the summer of 1967 a large coal depot opened at Westbury to serve all of Wiltshire except Swindon. It soon became redundant as most households changed to gas, oil, or electric central heating and coal fires became almost a thing of the past. Many of the sidings south of the station are today used by Mendip Rail stone trains. Westbury locomotive depot closed in April 1993, latterly servicing Trainload Freight locomotives, it was demolished in December 1993.

Bradford on Avon circa 1890. (Author's collection)

The Elizabethan-style Bradford on Avon station was re-named from just Bradford in January 1899. In 1852 George Spencer granted a patent for rubber springs for railway rolling stock, set up a rubber works at Bradford on Avon. His three sons all served their apprenticeship with Samuel Johnson, the Midland Railway locomotive, carriage and wagon superintendent. Care of the environment is not new. A land owner at Bradford on Avon got the WSWR to agree that embankments crossing his land should be planted by that company at the proper season next after their construction, with ornamental shrubs or evergreens, and protected, and from time to time renewed. In 1923 the LMS initiated a lorry service from Bath to the Bradford on Avon and Trowbridge area, receiving offices being opened in these two towns. The GWR countered this threat by introducing a van attached to passenger trains.

The LMS goods and parcels receiving office at Bradford on Avon. (Author's collection)

Avoncliff Halt opened 9 July 1906 immediately east of the aqueduct, is still open as narrow, steep lanes prevent easy road access to the hamlet. The next station on the line, Freshford, is in Somerset, but the line returns to Wiltshire before arriving at Limpley Stoke station, formerly the junction of the line to Camerton opened in 1910. Between Limpley Stoke and Freshford were exchange sidings for sorting the coal wagons. Senior boys of the nearby Monkton Combe School were allowed to bathe in the Avon. No costumes

(Left) 72XX class 2-8-2T No 7202 passes beneath the Kennet & Avon Canal at Avoncliff 23 May 1959 with a down coal train. (R. E. Toop)

(Right) 4-6-0 No 5942 *Doldowlod Hall* enters Limpley Stoke with a Bristol to Westbury stopping train 3 May 1958. (R. E. Toop)

were worn, so on the shout of 'Train', to preserve decency, everyone out of the water jumped in.

Westbury to Salisbury

The first mention of a railway between Westbury and Salisbury was in the 1820s when William James projected and surveyed a horse-worked line from Bristol to Salisbury and Southampton, but the idea proved abortive, then in 1845 the WSWR produced a different scheme. The GWR took over the rather moribund WSWR and opened the line Westbury to Warminster 9 September 1851. The local press grew very excited:

> 'Twas no partial festival, carried out in a patch of the place – the whole town rejoiced, from the crown of its head to the sole of its foot – it throbbed with as much emotion as though it felt that England at large had its eye on their proceedings – nay that 'all Europe, and part of Asia Minor were observing it'.

The previous evening, passengers entering the Warminster bus at Westbury were given a handbill announcing rustic sports – catching a pig with a greasy tail; climbing a greased pole to win a ham off the top, and donkey racing.

At 5.00am on 9 September cannons sounded. Rather later in the day a grand procession of 1,300 children followed by five or six wagon loads of babies too young to walk and too old to be left out of the proceedings, plus clergy of various denominations, marched to the station accompanied by bands. There were about 3,000 spectators and all formed lines either side of the track to await the arrival of the first down train.

The first train was hauled into Warminster by *Sagittarius*, built by Rothwell & Company at Bolton, Lancashire, ten years earlier. The engine was decorated with laurel and as it entered the station the band struck up 'The

Warminster station circa 1860. The train shed can be seen beyond the station offices. (Author's collection)

The main approach to Warminster station 19 September 1986. (Author)

The broad gauge 0-6-0 *Nemesis*, built 1855 and withdrawn 1877, at Warminster in 1874 immediately prior to narrowing the gauge. (Author's collection)

Warminster, view down circa 1910. Notice the train shed beyond the footbridge. (M. J. Tozer collection)

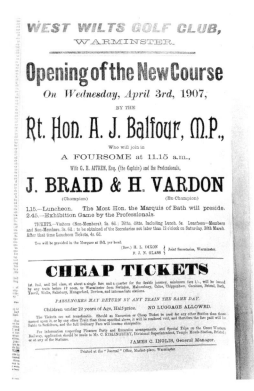

Conquering Hero'. The railway directors in the train seemed surprised to see the huge crowds as they only expected a few flags and a cheer or two. The line was extended to Salisbury on 30 June 1856 'without the usual formalities', and converted to standard gauge in June 1874. Warminster station platform was a foot too low and was lifted by jacks to the standard height, after which the whole station, (which was of timber construction), was also raised. Queen Victoria, Prince Albert and their children travelled over the line on 15 August 1856 en route from Plymouth to Osborne House on the Isle of Wight.

With the opening of the Severn Tunnel in 1886 the line became part of an important route for trains carrying coal from the South Wales pits to steamers at Southampton requiring coaling. Trains of as many as 36 coal wagons were worked up the bank from Bradford on Avon to Warminster, three locomotives being required to overcome the maximum gradient of 1 in 70. Sometimes a heavy train was divided at Westbury and worked in two halves up the bank to Warminster, the engine returning for the second part. Other trains had the assistance of a banking engine and Upton Scudamore signal box was opened in December 1900 at the head of the bank, to save the banker having to work through to Warminster. Additionally breaking Westbury to Warminster into two sections reduced line occupation.

In 1896 a Cardiff to Portsmouth passenger service was inaugurated which linked five ports: Cardiff, Newport, Bristol, Southampton and Portsmouth.

56XX class 0-6-2T
No 6618 leaves
Westbury with a
coal train for
Salisbury, starting
the climb of Upton
Scudamore Bank,
23 April 1955. It is
assisted in the rear
by sister engine No
5689. (R. E. Toop)

Until 1901 the line between Warminster and Salisbury was single track with 3 mph slacks at crossing stations for staff exchange by hand. Because of the increased traffic, freight, mineral and passenger, this had become unacceptable and doubling essential. Fortunately when the line was first constructed the engineer had the foresight to make bridges and earthworks wide enough for double track, so this task was carried out relatively easily.

Traffic on the line also increased when in 1895 the War Department purchased acres of land in the area for military training. The First World War caused new sidings and loading platforms to be built at Westbury and Warminster and in July 1916, the movement of the 60th (London) Division from camps near Warminster, Heytesbury and Codford to Southampton, involved the running of 88 special trains from these stations. Tank loading platforms were brought into use at Warminster in 1939.

In 1928 the GWR started its own lorry service from Warminster as it proved cheaper than using the local carter.

Dilton Marsh Platform was opened 1 June 1937, its interesting features being that the platforms were staggered and passengers entraining there had to purchase their rail tickets from a nearby house. In 1941-2 so many servicemen used the trains that a girl who lived at Dilton Marsh only travelled

Dilton Marsh Halt circa 1960.   (Lens of Sutton)

The shortened Dilton Marsh Halt 4 June 1993. Its surface is metal.   (Author)

to Trowbridge High School Tuesdays to Thursdays in order to release travelling space on the train. She was given plenty of homework to make up so her education did not suffer. In later years the platform was reduced to one coach length – 15m and its wooden surface covered with aluminium panels. These were stolen on 30 September 1988. In due course new safety regulations insisted that the platforms would have to be replaced by those of 58m to match the length of the longest train which called there. The cost of this would have been extravagant to cater for the 15 or so passengers who used it daily. Sense prevailed, the Department of Transport allowed an exception to be made and the new concrete platform was just 15m in length. A plaque bearing Sir John Betjeman's poem 'Dilton Marsh Halt' was displayed on the platform shelters when the rebuilt halt as opened on 30 April 1994 by his daughter Candida Lycett Green.

Langford, between Wylye and Wishford, closed as early as October 1857. Stockton Crossing between Codford and Wylye opened for use by workmen after 1907, was in use in July 1915 but closed later that year. The closure to passengers of all stations between Warminster and Salisbury occurred on 19 September 1955 and at the time made it one of the longest stretches of main line in the country without any passenger facilities.

Wilton Sheep Fair was held at a ground adjacent to the LSWR station, but sheep were removed by both railways. It was reputed to be the largest sheep fair in the country. In 1934 2,130 sheep were entered and 355 head of cattle.

The rebuilt Dilton Marsh Halt 2 September 1994. John Betjeman's poem 'Dilton Marsh Halt' is displayed at the end of the shelter. (Author)

A GWR 4-4-0 heads a four coach LSWR set at Heytesbury circa 1905. Notice the creeper trained to the end wall of the station building. The goods shed is spacious. (Author's collection)

Heytesbury view up circa 1950.   (Author's collection)

Codford, view down circa 1907. Signalman W. G. Pope stands at the foot of the steps.   (E. Notley)

Standard Goods 0-6-0 No 514 at Codford circa 1914.   (Gerald Quartley collection)

Codford, view down.   (Author's collection)

A down coal train passes Wylye circa 1905.(Author's collection)

Wylye, view up circa 1950. The gentlemen's cast iron urinal stands immediately beyond the station building.
(Lens of Sutton)

Wishford, view up circa 1955. The GWR lower quadrant signal has been replaced with a SR upper quadrant. (Lens of Sutton)

Wishford, view down circa 1955. (Lens of Sutton)

Station master Wilfred Talbot at Wishford circa 1955. (Author's collection)

Wilton, view down. The pointwork is interesting. (Lens of Sutton)

An ex-LMS Class 8 2-8-0 No 48431 of 82F shed (Bath, Green Park), heads a down train at Wilton 8 April 1964. No 48431 was built at Swindon in 1944 and initially loaned to the GWR. (Author)

Sheep from Wilton Fair being loaded in May 1934. (Charles E. Brown)

When the line opened in 1856 only a little traffic was transferred at Salisbury between the LSWR and the GWR, the companies preferring to exchange at Basingstoke. Even following the gauge conversion through traffic must have been light as it was not until three years later that the LSWR and GWR agreed to lay a connecting siding, each paying half the cost of £80. It was in use by February 1878.

The GWR terminus at Salisbury was designed by Brunel. The train shed had a glazed roof with smoke hood above the down platform road – it was unnecessary for the up road as here a locomotive stood in the open air at the other end of the train. The brick built offices were set at right angles to the track. The station closed to passengers 12 September 1932 as all except two

The GWR engine shed at Salisbury circa 1898. The LSWR station is on the right. The rails in the yard are spiked directly to the sleepers. In 1899 this stone-built shed was replaced by a brick three-road shed. (Author's collection)

The GWR locomotive shed at Salisbury which opened in 1899 and closed November 1950. (Author's collection)

Bulldog class 4-4-0 No 3329 *Mars* outside Salisbury passenger station circa 1929. A horse box stands on a middle road. (Author's collection)

The interior of the GWR terminus at Salisbury, 1925. Notice the ducting to collect smoke from incoming engines. Three of the roads are of chaired track, but one of the middle roads is of bridge rail. (Author's collection)

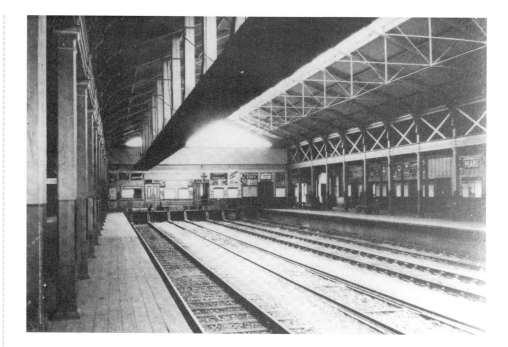

The exterior of the former GWR Salisbury terminus circa 1955. (Lens of Sutton)

Badminton class 4-4-0 No 4103 *Bessborough* at Salisbury with a through train from the SR, 31 May 1929. (H. C. Casserley)

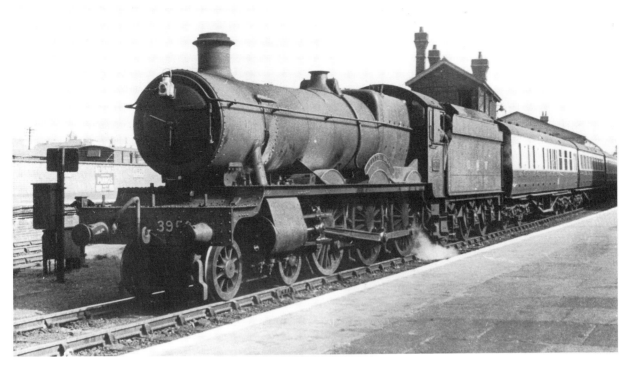

trains on the line worked beyond Salisbury to Southampton, Portsmouth or Brighton so terminating GWR trains were also diverted to the SR station. The former GWR passenger terminus was relegated to goods use until early 1991. It is Grade 2 listed.

A GWR engine taking over a train from the SR occasionally experienced difficulty because the GWR pressure for the vacuum brake was 25 in and the SR had a standard of 21 in. When the brakes were applied it was sometimes difficult to get them off, as if the coaches had been working on the SR for some time, only the lower part of the brake cylinders was smooth and shiny, the upper part being rusty and so sometimes the pistons would not free.

LSWR carriage and wagon examiners checked wagons entering their railway and any deemed unfit to travel were sent back to the GWR with the GWR transfer engine. Those needing repair but able to travel, were sent forward with load, but were marked for repair by the GWR. Likewise the GWR inspected wagons arriving from the LSWR.

LNER B12 class 4-6-0s worked ambulance trains during WW2 as they had the availability to travel over almost any line. A GWR 66XX class 0-6-2T was banking such a train up the gradient at Upton Scudamore. The B12 driver ignored the Automatic Train Control ramp at 'Danger', so the air brake was suddenly applied automatically. The 66XX, unaware of the situation, kept on pushing and some of the wounded were bumped to the floor.

The Berks & Hants Extension Railway: Bedwyn to Westbury

In 1845 Brunel planned a railway from Hungerford to Devizes and Westbury, which it was hoped would eventually reach Exeter by a more direct route than

The 10.35am Portsmouth to Cardiff at Salisbury 13 March 1948, worked by 4-6-0 No 3950 *Garth Hall*, an oil-burner. Its oil tank can be seen protruding above the tender. (Author's collection)

A down express east of Savernake Low Level: Wolfhall Junction signal box stands beside the sixth coach. (M. J. Tozer collection)

the existing one via Bristol. This new line displeased the townsfolk of Devizes who were rather peeved at being placed at the end of a 2½ mile subsidiary line and felt they should be on the main line.

The following year the GWR presented plans to Parliament for the necessary Act to be passed, but found itself opposed by the Kennet & Avon Canal Company which had planned its own line alongside the canal. The GWR bill failed to get through Parliament.

The following year, 1847, the citizens of Devizes asked Parliament to 'direct' the GWR to bring the line through the town as it would only have added 1½ miles to the length of the route. This petition was described as the product of 'a parcel of country-bred, though somewhat influential and persevering grumblers' and the Lords ordered the petition to lie on the table.

The GWR obtained its Act for the direct railway to Exeter in 1848, but failed to build the railway as the aftermath of the Railway Mania had made it impossible to raise money.

The Berks & Hants Railway had been opened to Hungerford on 21 December 1847 and the Devizes branch of the WSWR on 1 July 1857 leaving a gap of only 24½ miles between.

Thus in 1856 a local committee which had been appointed to consider the best means of constructing a railway between Devizes and Hungerford, recommended a line via Pewsey and Burbage. They stated that it would be 1¾ miles shorter than the alternative line via Marlborough, the gradients would be easier and it was more likely to be developed as a through line to the west. Building costs would be reduced by £35,000 and a first class station would be erected at Burbage for Marlborough traffic.

The Act was passed on 13 August 1859 authorising a capital of £298,000 and loans of £99,000. It was rather curious that it should be called the Berks

& Hants Extension Railway as it did not enter Hampshire and only two miles of line passed through Berkshire and most of the route was in Wiltshire!

The railway was built relatively cheaply as few earthworks were needed, mainly a deep cutting near Hungerford and a 190 yd long tunnel at Devizes. The cost of the line, including stations at Bedwyn, Savernake, Pewsey and Woodborough, did not exceed £240,000. The GWR promised to work the line.

The 24½ miles of broad gauge single line were opened formally on 4 November 1862 and to the public a week later on 11 November. For the first 20 years only four trains ran each way between Hungerford and Devizes, taking an average time of 70 minutes for the journey. A horse bus connected Marlborough with the railway at Savernake and a new section of road made to shorten the journey.

To save on capital cost, Savernake had a passing loop but no down platform, so when two passenger trains were required to pass there, one had to reverse into the loop, a rather a tricky procedure as the station was situated on a summit. Within a few years additional loops were opened at Bedwyn, Pewsey and Woodborough and disc block telegraph instruments installed to make the line safer. It was converted to standard gauge between 27 and 30 June 1874. The Berks & Hants Extension Railway had its own secretary and office at Devizes and enjoyed moderate prosperity until it was taken over by the GWR on 1 July 1882.

As mentioned earlier, critics of the GWR claimed that its initials stood for 'Great Way Round' and certainly some of its routes like that from Reading to Taunton via Swindon and Bristol were circuitous. Thus on 31 July 1894 the Stert to Westbury Act was passed for a direct line between Stert, 1½ miles west of Patney & Chirton station, to the existing WSWR at Westbury which was to be used as far as Castle Cary (in Somerset) from whence a new line would be built to reach Taunton.

By the end of 1899 double track working was opened between Hungerford and Woodborough and the Stert–Westbury cut-off was nearing completion. Weak underline bridges were rebuilt or strengthened. Between Hungerford and Savernake the Kennet & Avon Canal was so close that the desired re-alignment on easier curves befitting a main line was not possible. Construction was carried out by Messrs Pauling whose founder George Pauling collaborated with Cecil Rhodes in building much of the Cape to Cairo railway.

Bedwyn station originally had a single storey brick office building in Elizabethan style with a tall roof. This has now been demolished and replaced by a 'bus shelter' type structure, nevertheless today Bedwyn has a much better train service. In the 1950s only 8 trains called daily, but from the early 1960s Bedwyn became a terminus for some trains commencing at Paddington. Initially they used the former loading dock siding at the east end of the up platform, but then on 9 November 1976 this was closed and a new layover siding opened at west of the station. Today it enjoys a service of 16 trains daily.

In 1915 a pair of blue tits selected as their nesting site the hollow interior of a cast iron platform lamp post at Bedwyn. (Author's collection)

View down from Bedwyn station to No 165106 standing in the refuge siding between working the 12.28 from Paddington and the 14.24 to Paddington, 10 August 2001.   (Author)

DMU No 165106 draws into the up platform at Bedwyn having come from the refuge siding to form the 14.24 to Paddington, 10 August 2001.   (Author)

4-6-0 No 5096 *Bridgwater Castle* heads the 11.22am Bristol to Reading via Devizes express at Savernake Low Level on Monday 4 September 1939 – the first full day of the Second World War. This view was taken from Savernake West signal box. (E. J. M. Hayward)

A down express approaches Savernake Low Level. Savernake East signal box stands above the entrance to the Kennet & Avon Canal tunnel below the station. (M. J. Tozer collection)

Savernake Low Level view down. (S. Apperley)

The red brick Savernake Low Level station had a crisscross pattern of lighter coloured bricks. in the end walls. The station was at the summit of the line, 463 ft above sea level. The station was interesting for the fact that the Kennet & Avon Canal ran below its platforms in a 502 yd long tunnel. The station closed to passengers 18 April 1966 when the local passenger service was withdrawn.

Three quarters of a mile to the west, Burbage Wharf Siding offered exchange of goods between rail, canal and road until closure on 10 November 1947. Wootton Rivers Halt opened 24 September 1928 and closed 18 April 1966. Pewsey has an attractive station building in pink brick. It was renovated in 1984 and the timber shelter on the up platform replaced with a brick structure matching the style of the building on the opposite platform. Today 12 down and 9 up trains call. Circa 1930 snowdrops were collected

Wootton Rivers Halt c 1930: up view from the signal box. (Author's collection)

in local woods, packed in boxes and sent to the London market. Manningford Halt opened 20 June 1932 and closed 18 April 1966.

Woodborough had a smaller station building than the others on the line, but its ends were relieved with crosses in light brick. The local saw mill despatched considerable quantities of timber from the station. During the First World War, aircraft divided into sections arrived by rail from Filton, Bristol and taken by steam lorry to the flying field at Upavon for re-assembly. The station closed to passengers on 18 April 1966, but its loops were extended in April 1979.

The picturesque ticket office for Wootton Rivers Halt, circa 1940. (Author's collection)

Pewsey, view down circa 1910, showing the signal box which was replaced on 6 February 1923. (Author's collection)

Woodborough,
view down 29
September 1962.
(Author)

The 11.05am Westbury to Newbury approaches Pewsey 29 September 1962. This signal box opened 6 February 1923 and closed 2 May 1966. (Author)

The 6th Manchester Regiment detraining at Patney & Chirton in 1910 for West Down, South Camp. This military platform opened 1 August 1909. (Author's collection)

The main line platforms at Patney & Chirton, view down 19 April 1963. (Author)

Patney & Chirton did not receive a station until 29 July 1900 when it was required as an exchange station when the Stert and Westbury cut-off opened. Initially it was named Patney Bridge, but as this caused confusion with Putney Bridge of Boat Race fame, it was changed to Patney & Chirton. The red brick buildings were of the standard GWR design for the period. In July 1909 a military platform was added north of the passenger station in order to cater for a major Territorial Army exercise that year which used no less than 140 trains. This military platform was used in both World Wars, but dismantled in the early fifties. The station closed to passengers on 18 April 1966.

4-6-0 No 7029 *Clun Castle* heads a Stephenson Locomotive Society special at Patney & Chirton 24 January 1965. (Author's collection)

The 120 yd long Lavington Viaduct is crossed just east of Lavington, opened on 1 October 1900 to serve Market Lavington and West Lavington, but was actually nearer Littleton Pannell. It was in the usual GWR style of the period. Sited on an embankment of made ground, for lightness the platforms were largely of timber. On the up side a military siding was added 22 December 1914 and lengthened into a loop 30 July 1944, but taken out of use 27 September 1964. The station closed to passengers 18 April 1966.

Lavington, view west 19 April 1963. (Author)

Lavington, view up showing the goods shed, left. (Author's collection)

Blanketing work on the up track, Edington & Bratton, autumn 1951. (Author's collection)

4-6-0 No 4933 *Himley Hall* draws an up express through Edington & Bratton circa 1955. The platform edging stones have been removed and some can be seen stacked on the right. (T. J. Saunders)

An auto coach leading the last train to Westbury from Edington & Bratton 3 November 1952. (T. J. Saunders)

Edington & Bratton also opened to passengers on 1 October 1900. By the 1930s ticket sales averaged only three daily and it was closed to passengers 3 November 1952, though remained open for goods until 25 March 1963. Beyond are the Westbury Cement Works sidings and at Heywood Junction the Westbury Avoiding Line leaves the old line through Westbury. The double track Hawkeridge Loop was opened 14 July 1942 to allow direct running from Trowbridge towards Patney & Chirton.

Fairwood Junction, Westbury: 4-6-0 No 7924 *Thornycroft Hall* heads a Paddington to Weymouth train 23 April 1955. (R. E. Toop)

Pans Lane Halt view up circa 1955. A permanent way hut is on the right. (T. J. Saunders)

Patney & Chirton to Holt Junction

The WSWR branch from Holt Junction to Devizes opened on 1 July 1857 with no intermediate stations. The *Devizes Gazette* reported that: '...hundreds flocked to the station to see the first train leave at 7.4am and many spent the day travelling backwards and forwards between Devizes and Holt for the sheer joy of it.' Seend station opened in September 1858.

From Patney & Chirton the Devizes branch ran parallel with the main line for 1¼ miles before curving northwards. Pans Lane Bridge Halt opened 4 March 1929 ('Bridge' was later deleted), principally to serve Devizes Isolation Hospital and the Wilts United Dairies' factory. As push-pull trains used on the line needed no run-round facilities, a few services terminated and started at Pans Lane. The 208 ft long platform was also called at by some through trains to and from London, passengers wishing to alight were instructed to travel in the last two coaches. Pans Lane closed 6 October 1941 as a Second World War economy, though trains still called when required. The service was resumed after the war. The halt closed 18 April 1966.

4-6-0 No 5973 *Rolleston Hall* enters Devizes Tunnel with a four coach down express circa 1955. (T. J. Saunders)

The line passed through the 190 yd long Devizes Tunnel, now used for rifle shooting, and emerged into Devizes station. The original single platform was covered by a train shed, while the offices were of Bath stone. The conversion to standard gauge on 28 June 1874 offered extra space for a new island down platform. In 1910-11 the train shed was replaced with platform canopies. Goods facilities were extensive. Station water was supplied from

the Kennet & Avon Canal which had been purchased by the GWR 30 June 1852. Beyond Devizes the line descended at 1 in 52. The original Fish Bridge of wrought iron girders across the A361, in 1901 was replaced by a steel girder bridge with a span of 110 ft.

4-6-0 No 7914 *Lleweni Hall* leaves Devizes Tunnel with a down stopping train. (T. J. Saunders)

A 0-6-0PT approaches Devizes with a down pick-up goods circa 1955. (T. J. Saunders)

Devizes circa 1905 showing the train shed beyond the footbridge. (Author's collection)

Some members of staff at Devizes in 1947: Leading goods Porter Bob Lewis at the rear and left to right: Guard Sid Woolacock, Shunter Percy Vines and Goods Porter Clack. (Percy Vines)

Devizes station master Douglas Taylor circa 1955. The glass in the canopy gives the platform light.
(Author's collection)

Devizes view up circa 1955: military ambulances on Bedford chassis are on some of the well wagons towards the rear.
(Author's collection)

The Fish Bridge carries the railway across the A361 west of Devizes. (T. J. Saunders)

4-6-0 No 5928 *Haddon Hall* with a down train circa 1957 west of Devizes where the line crosses the Kennet & Avon Canal. (T. J. Saunders)

Bromham & Rowde Halt opened 22 February 1909. Immediately to the east was a goods loop while a siding served Seend Brick Works and saw mill. Produce from Bromham market gardens was despatched as was sugar beet. Milk traffic was important, 62,670 full churns being sent from the halt in

Bromham & Rowde Halt shortly after opening on 22 February 1909, view up.   (Author's collection)

Bromham & Rowde Halt, view up circa 1955. Beyond the corrugated iron pagoda is a canopy for sheltering milk churns from the sun. A wooden booking office is at the far end of the platform. (T. J. Saunders)

1926 earning an income of £4,600. It closed with all other stations on the line on the withdrawal of passenger services 18 April 1966.

The original Seend station was replaced by a GWR structure 30 August 1908 when a down platform was added. For much of the station's life, the iron works, or iron ore production, provided traffic.

Furnaces at Seend Iron Works under construction circa 1868. The six and four wheel iron-sided GWR wagons are being moved by horses. (Author's collection)

Seend, view up shortly after the signal box was opened on 30 August 1908. Beyond the over bridge, a siding to the right was served by a tramway from Seend Iron Mines. (Author's collection)

An up stopping train hauled by a 0-6-0PT enters Seend circa 1957. The down loop was taken out of use on 10 June 1956.
(T. J. Saunders)

The office building
on the up platform,
Seend circa 1955.
(T. J. Saunders)

4-6-0 No 4085
Berkeley Castle
with a down train
crosses an up train
at Seend circa
1955. The
platforms are
signalled for bi-
directional running.
The left signal post
is of concrete and
that on the right,
timber.
(T. J. Saunders)

57XX class 0-6-
0PT No 5781
approaches Seend
with an up auto
train circa 1955.
(T. J. Saunders)

Seend station seen
through the cab
window of a DMU
circa 1965.
(D. Payne)

Milk was another important commodity. Semington Halt opened on 1
October 1906 with the introduction of rail motor services from Trowbridge
– Devizes – Patney & Chirton. The platform at Semington was of sub-
standard height and the rail motor conductor was required to lower the coach
steps.

Until bridge strengthening works in 1938, Castle class locomotives were
prohibited from using the line, but from that year one express hauled by a
Castle worked daily to and from Bristol via Devizes and Newbury. The line

Semington Halt viewed from a DMU.   (T. J. Saunders)

Holt Junction circa 1965. The branch to Devizes curves right and the line to Chippenham is straight ahead.
(T. J. Saunders)

experienced heavy traffic during Tidworth Tattoo with trains from Bristol and South Wales.

A tragic event occurred near the Fish Bridge on 7 June 1889. Augustus Keeling, who had previously experienced mental problems, fell in love with Emily Lister, headmistress of Devizes British School. Embarrassed by his courtship, at half-term she decided to visit her parents in Birmingham.

Having bought a ticket to Seend, Augustus entered her compartment and asked for money. When she refused, he fired two shots into her head which fortunately did not penetrate her skull. As she leaned out of the window to shout for help, he grabbed her by the feet and pushed her out. The train was stopped near the gate to the brickyard. Before it came to a halt Augustus leapt from the train, but fell beneath it and was fatally injured.

The GWR Marlborough Branch

In coaching days Marlborough was an important stopping place on the London to Bath run, but the opening of the GWR in 1841 brought to an end this service and affected the lives of inn keepers, shop keepers, stablemen and horse feed suppliers. The opening of Marlborough College in 1843 helped alleviate unemployment. At the end of each term boys walked 12 miles to the railway at Swindon, or 11 miles to Hungerford.

An Act for building a broad gauge line from Savernake to Marlborough received Royal Assent on 22 July 1861 and contractor John Knight of Newbury began work in January 1863. On 30 March 1864 when carrying out his inspection of the completed line, the train carrying Colonel Rich stalled so many times on the gradients of 1 in 58 that rumour had it that people got out and pushed.

Savernake, Low Level 2 September 1961: N class 2-6-0 No 31810 heads the 4.52pm Swindon Town to Andover Junction and 57XX class 0-6-0PT No 9721 stands in the bay platform with the 5.33pm to Marlborough. (Author's collection)

Marlborough High Level station 17 April 1961.   (Author)

20hp Milnes-Daimler GWR bus to Calne at Marlborough High Level station circa 1908.   (Author's collection)

The line opened to the public on 14 April 1864, a horse bus connecting with Calne. By 1870 a dividend of 6 per cent was declared. The railway was closed for conversion to standard gauge on 27 June 1874, reopening on 1 July. The branch, worked by the GWR, became part of that company in July 1896.

At Marlborough it used what became known as the High Level station, as opposed to the Midland & South Western Junction Railway's Low Level station which came on the scene later (see page 126). A single storey building in 'contemporary Gothic' style, it was carried out in red brick relieved by stone. A canopy sheltered the platform for the length of the building. Due to reorganisation following the amalgamation of the MSWJR, Marlborough High Level closed to passengers 6 March 1933, all passengers using the Low Level station. On 10 October 1904 the GWR inaugurated a bus service to Calne. It was withdrawn 30 September 1913, but reinstated 24 July 1924. The GWR also ran bus services from Marlborough to Ramsbury, Aldbourne, Swindon, Hungerford, Newbury and Reading.

In 1881 the snow plough locomotive ran through the engine shed doors at Marlborough. (Author's collection)

A poster advertising the GWR Marlborough to Calne bus service which commenced 10 October 1904.

5 The London & South Western Railway

A S EARLY AS 1831 the London & Southampton Railway had planned a branch from Basingstoke to Bath and Bristol, though the London & Southampton lost its battle with the GWR to open rail communication to these cities.

The first standard gauge line in Wiltshire was the London & South Western Railway. The London & Southampton Railway, which was soon to become the LSWR, opened throughout on 11 May 1840. An extension from Bishopstoke (Eastleigh) to Salisbury was authorised by Parliament on 4 September 1844, but then the real problems started. Landowners proved obstructive regarding the LSWR taking over their property. Hoof & Hill won the building contract, but due to their late start because of the delay in freeing the land, they were unable to complete it by the early summer of 1846 as the contract specified. Labour was less easy to come by in the summer months due to farmers offering higher wages for harvesting. Joseph Locke, the line's engineer, was a humane man and did not ruin the contractors by insisting on the time limit, or hurting the farmers by offering higher wages. Eventually the line was open to Salisbury for coal and goods on 27 January 1847.

That day 2,000 citizens saw 0-6-0 No 52 *Rhinoceros* arrive with 23 wagons, three of these containing a total of 50 tons of coal for 'distressed persons', while another 50 tons arrived on the following train. The inaugural train was driven by Naylor, who usually had the honour of driving the LSWR Royal train.The Bishopstoke to Salisbury line opened for passengers on 1 March 1847, through passengers to and from London having to change at Bishopstoke, the fastest journey taking 3hr 50 min. The other station on this line in Wiltshire, other than Salisbury, is at Dean, sited just within the county, the boundary with Hampshire running immediately east of the station buildings, in fact the eastern section of both platforms are in Hampshire.

Ivatt Class
2 2-6-2T No
41320 shunting in
Milford Yard 22
January 1965.
(P. Strong)

The station used at Salisbury was not the one used today, but at Milford on the south eastern edge of the city. Milford closed to passengers 2 May 1859 when the present station in Fisherton Street opened, but Milford continued to be used by goods until 21 August 1967.

Although this route to London was better than nothing, Salisbury sought a direct line to the capital. On 13 August 1846 Royal Assent was given to the LSWR's Basingstoke & Salisbury Extension Act. Thomas Brassey was the contractor and to combat theft, four of his men were made special constables at the LSWR's expense. By October 1848, due to the Railway Mania, funds had expired and work temporarily abandoned. As the time allowed for building the railway had expired, a new Act was passed on 4 August 1853. Brassey restarted the work and was fortunate to enjoy dry weather to carry it out. The line opened to Andover 3 July 1854, but an Extension of Time Act was required on 14 August 1855 for the completion to Salisbury, the initial three years having proved insufficient. In order to reduce costs to a minimum, apart from over bridges and a viaduct at Monxton (Hampshire), all works were for just a single line. The line opened to Milford station on 2 May 1857 the only railway station in Wiltshire being Porton. Idmiston Halt opened 4 January 1943 to serve Porton Down Camp which employed both service and

Idmiston Halt view
down circa 1960.
(R. K. Blenkowe)

civilian personnel. Although a halt, it was staffed for much of the day. It
closed 9 September 1968.

Porton station opened initially with but a single track, but the line from
Salisbury was doubled on 1 June 1868 and eastwards on 1 July 1870. In the
1890s the War Department purchased an extensive area of Salisbury Plain so
Porton grew in importance. No platform awning was provided, but
passengers could shelter beneath part of a roof. Down passengers enjoyed a
timber shelter with a canopy. The station closed to freight on 10 September
1962 and to passengers on 9 September 1968.

Porton, view up
circa 1910, with
permanent way
gangers taking a
rest. LSWR signal
boxes had less glass
than many designs
– this had the
advantage that they
were warmer in
winter. (Author's
collection)

Having reached Salisbury, a westwards thrust was required to make the railway more profitable. The Salisbury & Yeovil Railway obtained its Act on 22 July 1848. The bill had a close escape from rejection. The official responsible for advertising the bill in a certain newspaper neglected to do so until the date required

C8 class 4-4-0 No 291 leaves the 443yd long Fisherton Tunnel with a Salisbury to Southampton train circa 1910. (Author's collection)

The Salisbury & Yeovil Railway coat of arms.

by Standing Orders had expired. This difficulty was surmounted by arranging with the journal's manager to print some copies of the issue containing the advertisement with an altered date and these fraudulent copies were produced to the Examiner of Private Bills. This official having been warned of the attempted deception, reported the matter to the House of Commons, at the same time certifying that the Standing Orders had not been complied with. The newspaper manager was summoned to attend and explain his conduct and confessed his delinquency. To everyone's surprise, the House resolved that the Standing Orders should be dispensed with.

When the first sod was cut in 1856 the railway had only £4 2s 4d in its bank account – rather a small sum to begin construction of a line which was to cost over £½ million, but eventually paid its shareholders a dividend of 14 per cent. This high figure was partly because of an attractive working agreement and partly because the directors, unlike those on some railways, avoided building feeder branches which often proved to be only expensive suckers, though to be fair, in the first half of the twentieth century quite a proportion of traffic came from flourishing branches such as Seaton and Exmouth.

Leslie & Davidson began work on the Salisbury & Yeovil Railway near Semley in 1856, but the following year they transferred the contract to Brassey. Navvies at Wilton were a riotous lot and the railway company was forced to pay the local authorities to employ constables to keep order. On 2 May 1859 the line was opened from Salisbury to Gillingham, Dorset, the last station on the line in Wiltshire being Semley. The line eventually opened to passenger traffic to Exeter on 18 June 1860, but goods did not run over any part of the line between Salisbury and Exeter until 1 September 1860.

In planning the route the engineer avoided costly earthworks which could not be paid for and tried to call at as many market towns as possible. Unfortunately the line went across the grain of the country, making its course a switchback and this had its effect on the locomotive department. It used specially designed engines with driving wheels at least 6 inches smaller in diameter than those employed between London and Salisbury. These smaller wheeled engines were much better at climbing. The usual way of working expresses between Salisbury and Exeter was to tear down a bank as fast as possible in order to get plenty of impetus to climb the next. The summit at Semley was 250 ft above Salisbury and about 200 ft higher than the next station, Gillingham, four miles distant.

The Salisbury & Yeovil Railway cost £12,513 per mile to build; doubling added an extra £3,884 giving a total of £16,397, which made it one of the cheapest lines in the country. The section from Yeovil to Exeter cost about twice this amount. When the railway was being built as far as Gillingham, 52 injured men were admitted to Salisbury Hospital, yet only six guineas of the costs were reimbursed by the contractor. Doubling the single line between Salisbury and Exeter was completed by 1 July 1870.

Traffic over the Salisbury & Yeovil Railway grew to such proportions that dividends rose to a height of 14 per cent and this to a company where, a few years earlier, shares were actually being given away by subscribers to escape impending calls.

In 1872 the LSWR offered £150 of its 5 per cent stock for £100 of Salisbury & Yeovil stock, but shareholders rejected it. In 1877 the offer of £260 of LSWR scrip for every £100 invested in the Salisbury & Yeovil was accepted and the company became vested in the LSWR from January 1878.

When opened, the new Salisbury station in Fisherton Street was of the single-sided pattern with one long platform, up trains logically used the London end and down trains the Exeter end. Additionally a bay platform was provided at the east end of the station. Salisbury was the last station Sir William Tite designed in Italianate style. A separate up platform was really required, but its potential site was covered by the GWR engine shed. An up platform was therefore built on the far side of Fisherton Street Bridge It opened on 19 August 1878. Expansion of services again caused difficulties

An L12 class 4-4-0 leaves Salisbury with an up express. The locomotive is on the approximate site of the 10 chain curve where No 421 left the rails (see page 154). The girders of Fisherton Street Bridge are in the foreground. (Author's collection)

Battle of Britain class 4-6-2 No 34051 *Winston Churchill* at Salisbury on 28 June 1954 carrying the Devon Belle headboard. (Revd Alan Newman)

Diesel electric No 10000 at Salisbury with the Atlantic Coast Express 26 April 1954. (David Crook)

BR Standard Class 9 2-10-0 No 92203 *Black Prince* at Salisbury with an up special 20 April 1975. The former GWR train shed is on the right. (W. H. Harbor)

and arrangements were made for the LSWR to demolish the GWR locomotive shed, replace it with a new building and offer sufficient land for three more platforms. A subway connected the platforms. The first new platform came into use in April 1902 when the up platform east of Fisherton Street Bridge closed. In conjunction with the 1902 remodelling, signalling at Salisbury was brought up to date. Instead of moving signals mechanically by wire, or points by rodding, a low pressure pneumatic system of 15 lb per square inch was utilised. Pressure was maintained by a compressor engine in a building separate from the signal box. The LSWR Guide for 1915 stated: 'Owing to Salisbury being a large locomotive station, special trains can at any time be supplied at thirty minutes' notice'.

The exterior of the down side of Salisbury station 8 July 1997. (Author)

The line was used by the Atlantic Coast Express, the most multi-portioned train the country, nine different sections for various destinations included in its formation. From 16 June 1947 the Pullman Devon Belle also ran over the line, with six coaches for Ilfracombe and four for Plymouth. As passengers were not picked up or set down at Salisbury, to avoid obstructing the platforms, the engine change was carried out at Wilton. An engine change was necessary as Waterloo to the first stop at Sidmouth Junction was too far to run without taking on water. The up Devon Belle simultaneously changed engines at Wilton. The Devon Belle was withdrawn at the end of summer 1954 through lack of patronage.

Much of the goods traffic west of Salisbury was for railway use – block loads of stone ballast from Meldon, Devon, while the principal coal traffic was that consumed by locomotives. The inclusion of goods trains in the same working diagrams as passenger trains was common, so that an engine working outwards on freight duty, might return home heading a passenger train. A nightly express goods train with automatic brakes throughout, ran from Exeter to Nine Elms, London. It was known as 'The Market', 'The Meat' or 'The Smithfield Flyer'. The only intermediate stations it called at were Templecombe and Salisbury.

As almost all trains had their engines changed at Salisbury, the locomotive depot was extensive. In 1902 the original depot comprising two 3-road sheds was replaced by a 10-road shed which in January 1947 was allocated a total of 83 locomotives. With the end of steam, it closed in July 1967. On 2 December 1942 new Merchant Navy Pacific No 21C10 *Blue Star*, hauled a 20-coach train from Waterloo to Exeter. This experiment lead the way to an engine of this class regularly hauling a 16-coach train to replace two trains which had run formerly, thus saving an engine, crew, fuel and allowing extra paths for wartime traffic.

The Salisbury to Exeter line was one of the first in England to see a diesel locomotive. About 1951 diesel-electric No 10202 made two trips daily totalling 687 miles, or 4,122 in a six-day week. Its average daily fuel consumption was approximately 760 gallons of fuel oil.

11 June 1993 a new depot opened to maintain 22 of the Class 159 Turbo diesel multiple-units introduced on the Waterloo to Exeter line. Unfortunately some passengers were confused by the plumbing arrangements on these new trains and pulled the emergency communication cord believing it to operate the toilet flush. The final regular locomotive hauled train called at Salisbury on 10 July 1993.

East of Wilton South, a crossover opened 28 October 1973 between the ex-GWR and LSWR lines enabling trains from Westbury to use the

Salisbury Traincare Depot 8 July 1997. (Author)

Two trains at Wilton, view down circa 1907. (Author's collection)

former LSWR tracks. The ex-GWR line eastwards to Salisbury was then lifted, apart from a length used as Quidhampton Siding.

Wilton was renamed Wilton South on 26 September 1949 to distinguish it from the ex-GWR station which had been renamed Wilton North. The station building at Wilton South was a typical Salisbury & Yeovil style in red brick with slated roof. The walls facing south and west were slate-hung to prevent the penetration of rain. The station was gas lit until closure. A plate girder footbridge was installed in 1896 to obviate passengers having the cross the line on the level, particularly dangerous in poor visibility due to a 30 chains radius curve. Passenger traffic at the station was generally light with a daily average of about 17 in 1963. Although Wilton had a population of 2,193, in the mid-thirties the station only issued about 1,000 tickets annually. It dealt with a fairly heavy trade in watercress. It closed to goods 6 July 1964, to passengers on 7 March 1966 (as were Dinton and Semley), and the line to Templecombe was singled 2 April 1967. Wilton signal box which closed on 29 November 1981 is now in use at Medstead & Four Marks station on the Mid Hants Railway.

Air Ministry sidings were opened south of Dinton station 11 June 1939 and closed 2 November 1994. The station building was the standard Salisbury & Yeovil design. The 5,000 passengers using Dinton in 1938 rose to 32,000 in 1943 and the number of wagons in the same period rose from 1,318 to almost 10,000. Dinton only enjoyed an average of 30 passengers daily in 1963. Watercress was despatched from the station. West of Dinton, in 1937 Chilmark Quarry was requisitioned by the Air Ministry for ammunition storage. The sidings were taken out of use in 1994.

Dinton view up circa 1905. Trees of this height are not often seen so close to the platform.   (Author's collection)

Dinton, view down 8 April 1964. In the distance BR Standard Class 5 4-6-0 No 73166 is shunting.   (Author)

BR Standard Class 5 4-6-0 No 73166 at Dinton 8 April 1964. (Author)

Tisbury station building was of the usual Salisbury & Yeovil design, but a substantial arc-roofed canopy was added in 1882 and a footbridge replaced a foot crossing in 1888. Tisbury booked 16,300 passengers in 1938 and 73,000 in 1943, the number of wagons in the same period rising from 5,000 to 24,000. An average of 110 passengers used the station daily in 1963, one reason being that it was conveniently sited. Freight despatched included agricultural machinery manufactured locally by F.J. Parmiter Sons. The modern flat-roofed signal box replaced a wooden cabin on 12 October 1958, but closed 5 February 1967. Although Wilton to Gillingham was singled in

S15 class 4-6-0 No 30842 near Tisbury with the 12.16 pm Templecombe to Bournemouth West via Salisbury, 4 August 1962. (Author)

Tisbury, view down circa 1960. The new signal box opened 12 October 1958 and closed 5 February 1967. (Lens of Sutton)

Tisbury, view up. (Lens of Sutton)

April 1967, to ease subsequent delays, a long reversible passing loop to the east of Tisbury was opened 24 March 1986 at a cost of £435,000. Although a passing loop actually at the station would have been a better option, this was impossible due to the land having been sold to Messrs Parmiter. The station platform was raised in 1992-3 to suit the Class 159 diesel multiple units. The booking office was also refurbished.

'Semley for Shaftesbury' was another standard Salisbury & Yeovil structure, but unlike some, privileged to have a canopy. It was sited at the summit of the 17 mile long gradient from Salisbury. Steep gradients precluded the line from actually reaching Shaftesbury, but in the early days it was served by a horse bus meeting all trains except the 7.03am. At the beginning and end of term, pupils of Clayesmore School used the station. In 1963 an average of 105 passengers used the station daily. It closed to passengers 7 March 1966. On Shaftesbury market day, beasts were driven 2½ miles down the road to the station. Although generally sent forward by scheduled trains, sometimes a special was required. Pit props were another local speciality.

Semley view up 8
April 1964. The
goods shed closed
5 April 1965.
(Author)

A wholesale milk depot was set up at Semley, primarily to serve the need of London. It opened in May 1875 and was the first to be established anywhere in the country. 2,500 gallons of milk were despatched daily in 1904. Pipes for loading milk into tank wagons, rather than churns, were installed in 1931. When a glut of milk was experienced in summer, any surplus milk was sent in tanks to factories at Bailey Gate (on the Somerset & Dorset Railway), or Hemyock (Devon), where it was made into butter, cheese, or milk powder.

Semley showing the
creamery at the
west end of the
station, 8 April
1964. Milk tanks
have replaced
churns and milk
vans. Notice that
pipes carry milk
across the road
from the creamery
to the station.
(Author)

The milk tanks were shunted by horses and to offer them a better foothold, the formation between the rails was ballasted with finer stone laid about six inches proud of the sleepers. Shunting horses were replaced by a locomotive in the 1940s. Milk traffic ceased in 1980. Beyond Semley the line descends at 1 in 100 to Blackmoor Vale and passes into Dorset.

Semley, view up circa 1910 showing the milk dock to the left of the locomotive. A horse box stands near the buffer stops. (Author's collection)

6 **Branches from the London & South Western Railway**

Salisbury Market House Railway

For more than a century the shortest standard gauge railway in Britain was a feature of the Salisbury scene.

The story really started back in 1856 when the WSWR opened its branch from Westbury to Salisbury. The citizens of Salisbury, concerned in case their market died out because of the distance from the station, proposed a rail link.

An Act of Parliament which received Royal Assent on 14 July 1856, permitted the Salisbury Market House Company to build a line and market, and to raise a capital of £12,000 for this purpose.

The interior of Salisbury Market House; a railway wagon can be seen on the left behind the pillars. (Author's collection)

The line was to be worked by the LSWR, which at that time was constructing a line from Basingstoke. The Market Railway required four bridges to span two streams, the Avon and the Mill Leat and brought railway wagons to within a few yards of the Market Square. The line was built by Thomas Brassey for £1,501 8s 8d. It opened in May 1859, probably on the 2nd when the LSWR inaugurated the present passenger station. The branch descended from the main line to ground level. Wagons were initially horse-drawn, but following a runaway in 1868, the line was adapted for locomotive working and in its latter years, only small engines were permitted to operate.

The Market House Railway never actually carried meat, fish and poultry as was originally envisaged. Instead it was primarily concerned with the transport of coal and barley to the malting which grew up on either side of the line and also carried traffic to and from the saw mill, together with cheese, wool and seeds. After the Second World War, coal for the Salisbury Electric Light & Supply Company, later part of the Southern Electricity Board, formed the principal traffic. This power station changed to oil in 1962.

The Market House itself measured 77ft by 174ft, with walls of red and white brick having a glass roof. A gallery was provided for storing corn two sacks deep. The building's pedimented façade was in Bath stone. Provision was made for a clock to be given by the then Mayor, if the building was completed during his term of office. The structure cost £2,887.

The Market House was opened on 24 May 1859 with a celebratory dinner. Within nine months of opening, sales of cheese, corn and wool, the commodities with which the building dealt, occupied all available space. The company paid its first dividend, 3½ per cent, in 1866. Subsequently 5 per cent was paid quite frequently until 1895 when revenue began to decline. The cheese traffic on the line ceased in 1903, corn traffic in 1913, while during the First World War the track inside the Market House was lifted. The seasonal wool market lasted until 1940 when only the corn market remained.

Despite the reduction of traffic, the company continued to pay respectable dividends – 5½ per cent in 1933 and 12½ per cent in the 1950s. Latterly British Railways managed and worked the line at a rent of £150 annually – £10 less than the LSWR charged 90 years before!

Following closure of the railway on 1 July 1964, the track was lifted in December. The company was wound up in 1965 by voluntary liquidation. Salisbury public library is now behind the façade.

The Salisbury & Dorset Junction Railway

Entrepreneurs spotted the need for a line linking Salisbury with Wimborne on the Southampton & Dorchester Railway. This idea was supported at a meeting held in Salisbury on 20 October 1860. Its Act was passed on 22 July 1861, but the first sod was not cut at Downton by Countess Nelson until 3 February 1864. Hopes for the anticipated opening in 1865 were shattered when the contractor, Garrett & Company, due to his insufficient financial backing, had his contract stopped on 22 September 1864. He was replaced by Henry Jackson. Financiers then lost interest in the project and this, coupled with the unusually wet winter of 1865-6 delayed the line's completion.

When Captain Tyler carried out the Board of Trade inspection in August 1866, he found that the works were below the new standard required, but luckily for the railway company, Jackson generously made these improvements at cost price. In order to finance this work, six shareholders lent £600 for three months. Unfortunately Tyler's re-inspection on 30 October 1866 required yet more work. Additional shares were issued and the LSWR agreed to complete the line and carry out the first year's maintenance.

The line opened on 20 December 1866, but the LSWR, which worked the line, was only able to pay £14 to the Salisbury & Dorset Junction Railway as its share of the income for the first six months. Part of the problem was blamed on 'the difficulties and delays which always arise in diverting from its old channels the long established traffic'. Fortunately things took a turn of the better and receipts rose from £4,981 in 1868 to £8,893 in 1875.

Downton, view towards Salisbury. The signal box was reduced to a ground frame 1 December 1922 and the right hand loop converted to a siding. (Author's collection)

T9 class 4-4-0 No 30707 enters Downton with a Salisbury to Bournemouth West train. The right hand platform is shelterless as the down loop became a siding in 1922. (Author's collection)

Downton, view towards Salisbury 2 May 1965. (D. Payne)

The LSWR was to blame for the fact that receipts were not even greater. It was in its best interests to send passengers the longer way round via its own route, thus increasing its receipts, rather than sending passengers on a more direct route via the Salisbury & Dorset Junction and having to share the income. Eventually the Salisbury & Dorset Junction shareholders realised their line was not going to be profitable, and sold it to the LSWR on 31 October 1882.

Only the northern part of the line was in Wiltshire, and the only station in the county was at Downton. Unlike some stations which were placed for the convenience of the railway, rather than of the passengers, it was located at the east end of the village. The main buildings were on the up platform, the down merely having a waiting shelter and shed. From 1903 an open ironwork bridge linked the platforms. It only held the status of a crossing station until 1 December 1922, as from that date the down loop became a wagon siding. In November 1936 to cope with increased pig movements, a new dock and pens were provided in the goods yard. The station closed to goods and passengers 4 May 1964

The line actually entered Wiltshire at Pile Bridge spanning the Avon a mile south of Downton station. The branch joined the Salisbury to Southampton line at Alderbury Junction four miles south-east of Salisbury. No public station was provided at the junction, but staff platforms were provided until 4 May 1964 when trains ceased to call.

7 The Midland & South Western Junction Railway

SWINDON IS ALMOST synonymous with the GWR, yet another railway dared run through its headquarters. This was the Midland & South Western Junction Railway. Projected as a trunk route, it opened as a local line, became an important through railway and finally finished as it began – a railway backwater.

The line was mooted back in the 1840s as the Manchester & Southampton Railway, but a shortage of capital prevented this grandiose scheme from coming to fruition. However the idea was not forgotten and partly resurrected when the Swindon, Marlborough & Andover Railway Act was passed on 21 July 1873, this Act giving running powers over the Marlborough Railway between Marlborough and Savernake.

The line's woes began on 28 July 1875 when the first sod was turned, the wheel of the barrow containing it and pushed by Lord Bruce, broke. More money was then wanted when work started on a 773 yard long tunnel at Swindon and then abandoned when a cheaper deviation was made to the west, works having stopped through lack of funds. An Extension of Time Act was passed 16 April 1878.

The contractors Watson, Smith, Watson Ltd began work the following year. A trial run between Swindon and Marlborough was made on 25 June 1881. As the first sod had been turned at Marlborough, to be fair, the opening ceremony was held at Swindon on 26 July 1881. Imaginatively, for the line's first August Bank Holiday Monday, ordinary services were suspended and special trains run every 1½ hours to take passengers to Marlborough so that they could enjoy picnics in Savernake Forest. Of the 1,400 passengers carried that day, 950 booked from Swindon. The railway's opening reduced the price of coal at Chiseldon by five shillings a ton.

Grafton to Andover opened on 1 May 1882, but the Board of Trade would not countenance the use of Marlborough as a junction station until certain improvements were carried out. These were made and on 3 February 1883 there was a ceremonial opening of the whole line from Swindon to Andover. It opened to the public on 5 February 1883 from which date all trains conveyed through coaches to Southampton.

The *Swindon Advertiser* of 10 February 1883 noted in its editorial that when the GWR had been the sole railway in the town then it:

> ...charged the utmost farthing for the accommodation it had afforded; but when there has been competition, when other railway systems have contended with it for the trade and patronage of a town or district, then the Great Western has lowered its rates and extended its facilities in a very marked manner.

To be economic the SMAR required to be part of a through route. The Swindon & Cheltenham Extension Railway was floated to link with the Midland Railway and the North, the Act being passed on 18 July 1881. Its metals did not actually reach Cheltenham, but from Andoversford powers were granted for running the rest of the distance over the Banbury & Cheltenham Direct Railway.

Watson, Smith, Watson, contractors for the SMAR, agreed to build the SCER and began work in the summer of 1882. In a letter of 2 October 1883 to the directors, they observed that the railway's name gave potential subscribers the idea that it was a purely local line. An attempt was made to get an Act for additional capital, make a working agreement with the SMAR and change the company's name, but these efforts failed.

Goods traffic began between the junction with the GWR at Rushey Platt, Swindon and Cirencester on 1 November 1883. Due to a slipping embankment, the line could not be opened to public passenger traffic. Eventually the problems was solved and the first public trains ran on 18 December 1883.

By an Act of 23 June 1884 the SMAR and the SCER amalgamated to form the Midland & South Western Junction Railway. By October 1884 the company's financial situation was in serious trouble. Train services were curtailed and some jobs combined. In November Watson, Smith, Watson at work on the extension north of Cirencester, were released from their contract and went bankrupt the following year. On 20 December 1884 the MSWJR went into receivership. the following April, the Metropolitan Carriage & Wagon Company threatened to repossess rolling stock until immediate payment was made. The directors instructed the MSWJR's locomotive engineer to select the most useful items of rolling stock to the value of £7,500 which had already been paid, and return the rest.

February 1888 saw the tender of Messrs Ridley & Whadcoat accepted for the completion of the line to Andoversford. The firm was modern and used steam excavators. The line eventually opened on 1 August 1891.

There was now every hope that the impecunious company could become an important through route, be worked profitably and go out of Receivership, in fact at one time, passengers could travel more quickly from Cheltenham to London via the MSWJR and Andover, than by the more direct Great Western Railway.

When E T Lawrence, the company secretary, met the newly appointed manager, Sam Fay, off the train at Cirencester in 1892, he said: 'Do you know this line is nearly bankrupt and there is not enough money in the bank to pay the staff at the end of the week?' Fay replied: 'Don't say that, I see great possibilities in this line.'

Although some weeks the position was so bad that Fay himself had to go to the various debtors to collect enough cash to pay the wages, the line flourished to such an extent that the Receiver was discharged in 1897. Fay did a marvellous job. Between 1894 and 1898 he increased traffic receipts by 73 per cent for an increase in expenditure of only 18 per cent. One great bugbear was that the MSWJR had to use the GWR's Marlborough branch between Marlborough and Savernake. The GWR disliked the intruder and used several ploys to delay its trains. In 1½ years 170 MSWJR trains were delayed for about half an hour and one train for no less than five hours.

To avoid these delays the MSWJR proposed a new line, the Marlborough & Grafton Railway, to link both sections of the MSWJR. The Act was passed on 7 August 1896 and Lucas & Aird's tender accepted. The 647yd long Marlborough Tunnel was bored so accurately that when the two headings met, the deviation was less than 3/8 inch. The line opened on 26 June 1898.

During both World Wars the MSWJR proved invaluable carrying military supplies to the channel ports and hospital trains with wounded from Southampton to the North. Drivers were sometimes so busy that they did not see their families for a fortnight at a time, occasionally working 24 hours non-stop.

The red light showed for the first time in December 1958 when trains were diverted from Cheltenham (Lansdown) station, where they connected with trains from the North, to Cheltenham (St James'). This meant that the line could only deal with local passenger traffic and this was not heavy enough to be economic. At the same time, the three express goods trains each way were withdrawn, leaving no regular goods trains between Andoversford and Cirencester.

The final blow came in 1961 when it was announced that passenger traffic would be withdrawn from 9 September and the Cirencester to Andoversford section closed completely.

Swindon to Cirencester, Swindon to Swindon Town, Andover to Ludgershall and Savernake to Marlborough remained open for freight. The Cirencester goods was withdrawn from 1 April 1964, but the line remained open for coal trains to Moredon power station. The line to Marlborough closed 7 September 1964; while Swindon Town and Moredon closed 31 December 1975, Andover to Ludgershall still remaining open.

Milk was a very important source of income for the MSWJR. A milk train left Cricklade with four loaded vans. At Blunsdon 60 churns were loaded, 20 to 25 more at Moredon and another van coupled on at Rushey Platt. More vans were added at Swindon Town. These were filled by the time the train reached Marlborough where more vans were added and one or two more joined the train at Savernake. It arrived at Andover with 17 loaded vans for the LSWR to take forward to Clapham Junction and Waterloo.

The MSWJR owned a very important branch line. Sam Fay's successor as general manager was James Purkess, appointed 4 April 1899. He was certainly the right choice as during his reign receipts increased by 50 per cent – no mean feat considering that Fay had managed the line so ably.

One of Purkkess's first acts was to seek an interview with the War Department regarding the construction of a railway between Ludgershall and a new military camp being established at Tidworth. The line was built under an agreement of 19 November 1900 between the MSWJR and the War Department, no Act being required since it was constructed solely on War Office land. It opened for manoeuvres on 8 July 1901. War Department goods were carried from 21 May 1902, public goods from 1 July 1902 and public passengers from 1 October 1902.

The seven roads in Tidworth yard held 290 wagons, or 10 trains of 12 coaches. Beyond the station the War Department had about 2½ miles of track worked by its own locomotives. Receipts at Tidworth station were the greatest on the MSWJR and the station was in charge of the railway's highest-ranking stationmaster. It was also the only station on the MSWJR lit by electricity. The county boundary ran through the station so while a passenger purchasing a ticket stood in Hampshire, the booking clerk on the other side of the ticket window was in Wiltshire.

The branch's most hectic days were pre-Second World War when the Tidworth Tattoo was held. Trains arrived from the GWR, LMS and SR and required very careful stabling to enable them to leave in the correct order. The

A MSWJR 0-6-0T and four coaches arrive at Tidworth. The board at the end of the station building advertises the White Star Line and the Japan British Exhibition. (Author's collection)

Tidworth circa 1960, a shadow of its former self. (Lens of Sutton)

branch passenger service was withdrawn on 19 September 1955 and the line closed completely 31 July 1963.

The first MSWJR station in Wiltshire was Ludgershall. Originally a simple double track crossing station, War Department needs required expansion to five wide platforms. Special traffic at Collingbourne station was racehorse traffic to and from stables and also agricultural machinery from Messrs Rawlings & Sons' works.

Collingbourne Kingston Halt, opened 1 April 1932, had sleeper-built platforms and tickets were purchased from a nearby house. Grafton station

London & North Western Railway six-wheel coaches have arrived at Ludgershall in 1906 with a contingent of troops. (Author's collection)

Troops and horses on the platform at Ludgershall circa 1906. A train of horse boxes is on the far left. The junction to Tidworth is behind the photographer. (Author's collection)

45XX class 2-6-2T No 5555 runs light engine through Ludgershall 17 April 1961. (Author)

BR Standard Class 4 2-6-4T No 80096 shunting at Ludgershall 29 April 1965. (Author)

Army diesel shunter No 8219 at Ludgershall 29 April 1965. (Author)

43XX class 2-6-0 No 5306 at Ludgershall with a Railway Correspondence & Travel Society special. (Author's collection)

South of Collingbourne, 45XX 2-6-2T No 5555 works a goods train to Ludgershall 17 April 1961. (Author)

Collingbourne, view down circa 1960. (Author's collection)

BR Standard Class 4 2-6-0 No 76028 at Collingbourne Kingston Halt with the 1.52pm Cheltenham to Andover 17 April 1961. (Author)

Grafton, view up circa 1960. (Lens of Sutton)

Grafton, view down 17 April 1960. (Author)

was of red brick. Three-quarters of a mile north of the station was a triangular junction, the straight line leading to Savernake High Level station, while the right hand Grafton Curve gave a through run towards Newbury. The High Level line almost immediately offered a line leading to Savernake Low Level.

The MSWJR's station (High Level was added to its name 1 July 1924), was approximately 200yd north of the Low Level station on a parallel line. The Marquis of Ailesbury had a private waiting room on the down platform.

43XX class 2-6-0 No 6309 heads a Swindon to Andover train at Grafton South Junction. The right hand curve leads towards Newbury. The signal box closed 11 September 1961. (Author's collection)

A down goods train passes through Savernake High Level circa 1958. (Author's collection)

View north towards Marlborough Tunnel 26 February 1965. The line on the left is from Savernake Low Level and the lifted track, right, was from Savernake High Level. (Author)

The temporary Marlborough West signal box brought into use when single line working was introduced through Marlborough Tunnel 26 July 1944 to 18 August 1946. (Author's collection)

As an economy measure the station closed to passengers 15 September 1958 and to goods 22 June 1959.

The fact that the GWR's Marlborough branch and the MSWJR were within sight of each other between Savernake and Marlborough, gave an opportunity for footplate crews to have unofficial races, the GWR usually winning as it used a two-coach train whereas MSWJR trains were longer. The fact that the two lines were so close allowed for an economy From 6 March 1933, the former GWR's Marlborough branch 1¾ miles north of Savernake was slewed into the ex-MSWJR's up line. Hence the three miles of former double track to Marlborough became two parallel single lines. The GWR's Marlborough High Level station was relegated to goods traffic use.

The MSWJR Marlborough Low Level station was blessed with a refreshment room. The next station, Ogbourne dealt with race horse traffic. Chiseldon Camp Halt, a sleeper-built platform, opened 1 December 1930. Chiseldon was another station which dealt with race horses.

Swindon Town station originally had two platforms, but was given a third in 1904-5. The line beyond descended at 1 in 75 to Rushey Platt which closed

Scooping a chalk fall from a cutting on the approach to Marlborough Tunnel circa August 1946.   (Author's collection)

0-6-0ST *A. J. Keeble*, the Dodsdown Brick Works locomotive at Marlborough MSWJR station.   (Author's collection)

MSWJR 4-4-0 No 8 at Marlborough with the 1.10pm South Express 1914.   (Author's collection)

A 4-4-0 enters
Marlborough circa
1914.   (Author's
collection)

The Cameronians on
manoeuvres in
September 1934 at
Marlborough Low
Level station, smoke
issuing from the
machine guns. The
up express is headed
by a 43XX class
2-6-0. To the left
near the signal box,
can be seen the
High Level station,
closed to passengers
just over a year
previously on
6 March 1933.
(Author's collection)

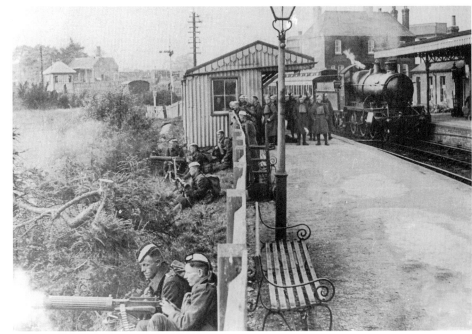

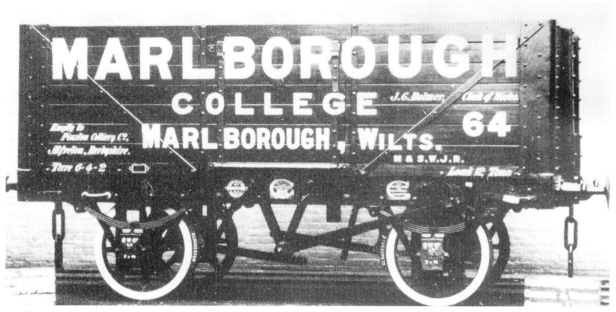

Marlborough College coal wagon No 64. It was probably the only member of the fleet. Painted purple-brown, it was built by the Gloucester Railway Carriage & Wagon Works in March 1907. (Author's collection)

A permanent way trolley and trailer on the up road at Marlborough Low Level 13 July 1961. The water tank at the High Level station can be seen to the right of the house. (R. E. Toop)

Marlborough Low Level 13 July 1961: U class 2-6-0 No 31809 works the 1.52pm Cheltenham to Andover and 57XX class 0-6-0PT No 9720 the 2.50pm Andover to Swindon. The group of schoolgirls returning home probably did not appreciate train travel. (R. E. Toop)

57XX class 0-6-0PT No 4697 at Marlborough Low Level with a train of permanent way sleepers 13 July 1961.
(R. E. Toop)

The private siding for the Ogbourne Racing Stables, circa 1898. It was brought into use June 1897.
(Author's collection)

Ogbourne, view down. This signal box closed 7 January 1943 and was replaced by another further north when the loop was extended on 7 January 1943.   (Lens of Sutton)

Chiseldon view down circa 1910. MSWJR sheet No 30 is draped over an object.   (Author's collection)

Chiseldon view up 17 April 1961. The signal box was rebuilt in 1942.   (Author)

MSWJR 2-6-0 No 16 at Swindon Town 1921. As GWR No 24 it enjoyed a moment of glory circa 1927 when a 'King'
failed west of Swindon. No 24 was uncoupled from a pick-up goods and headed the express into Swindon.
(Author's collection)

Ex-MSWJR 0-6-0
No 23 rebuilt as
GWR No 1007,
seen here at
Swindon Works 24
January 1937. It
was withdrawn in
June 1937. (S.
Miles Davey)

Duke class 4-4-0
No 3268 *Chough* -
an apt name -
stands at Swindon
Town with a down
train circa 1930.
(Author's
collection)

An 0-6-0PT stands
at Swindon Town 4
April 1959.
(Author's
collection)

Swindon Town, view up.   (Lens of Sutton)

Hymek diesel-hydraulic D7044 at Swindon Town 29 April 1965.   (Author)

The former MSWJR offices overlooking Swindon Town station on 17 April 1961.   (Author)

The interior of Rushey Platt signal box circa 1934.   (Author's collection)

Rushey Platt view south. An ex-MSWJR 0-6-0 rebuilt by the GWR heads a train towards Cirencester, while the branch from Swindon Junction joins on the left. (Author's collection)

Rushey Platt view towards Swindon Town. The branch from Swindon Junction is on the left together with the remains of Rushey Platt Low Level station, closed 1 October 1905. Rushey Platt signal box is in the centre of the photograph. (Author's collection)

The siding to Moredon Power Station 21 April 1965.   (Author)

Moredon ground frame box, right, 21 April 1965. (Author)

The restored station at Blunsdon 10 June 1989. (Author)

A goods train headed by a 0-6-0 enters Cricklade circa 1905. (Author's collection)

Cricklade view up 1935. A GWR Thornycroft lorry stands on the platform.   (Author's collection)

An Aberdare class 2-6-0 at Cricklade with a down goods, 1935.   (Author's collection)

Cricklade view down 6 May 1960. (Author)

The aftermath of the ammunition train explosion at Savernake 2 January 1946. (Author's collection)

to passengers on 1 October 1905. Just beyond it crossed the GWR main line to the west of Swindon Works. Moredon Platform opened 25 March 1913 principally for milk traffic, but closed 1 October 1932. Nearby was the electricity works served by sidings. Blunsdon opened on 1 September 1895 and dealt with milk and cattle feed, but saw few passengers so closed on 1 August 1937. Cricklade had two platforms and north of the station the line crossed the infant Thames by a span of 35ft and passed into Gloucestershire.

A heavy loss of life could have occurred on 2 January 1946. Ammunition was being transferred from lorries to railway wagons in the depot at Savernake Forest, when a violent explosion destroyed wagons and set others ablaze. Eight soldiers were killed and fires threatened not just the train being loaded, but a fully loaded train alongside.

Blunsdon view
north 10 June 1989
from the cab of a
Fowler diesel
locomotive.
(Author)

96 wagons containing 2,000 tons of explosives were threatened and had these been detonated, many lives would have been lost in nearby Marlborough.

Captain Kenneth Biggs personally uncoupled a blazing ammunition wagon and with another officer, pushed it to safety and extinguished the blaze. Biggs and Acting Staff Sergeant Rogerson worked through the night ensuring that fires in every burning wagon were extinguished and those burning too fiercely were pushed out of harm's way. 69 wagons were saved. Biggs and Rogerson were both awarded the George Cross.

Closure of most of the MSWJR in 1961 did not prove to be the end. A group of enthusiasts have resurrected part of the line as the Swindon & Cricklade Railway. From its headquarters at Blunsdon it is thrusting northwards towards Cricklade and extended to South Meadow Lane 25 May 2008.

8 Military Railways

SALISBURY PLAIN, a vast, largely uninhabited tract of country, being situated towards the south coast and thus fairly near the continent, was ideal for military training. The first camps were set up towards the end of the nineteenth century.

A Light Railway Order was granted on 28 September 1898 for the Amesbury & Military Camp Light Railway. Unlike most light railways, it had embankments and cuttings, rather than the line following the lie of the land. It also had chaired track, rather than the flat-bottomed variety with rail spiked directly to the sleepers and sufficient land was purchased to allow for doubling.

It opened to military traffic on 1 October 1901, to public goods on 26 April 1902 and passengers 2 June 1902, the first train carrying newspapers with the joyful headline that the South African War was over.

A Light Railway Order of 10 January 1903 authorised an extension from Amesbury to camps at Bulford and Sling. This was opened 1 June 1906.

As the junction near Newton Tony only offered a direct run to the east, on 8 August 1904 the LSWR constructed a line which burrowed below the main line to give additionally a through run from the branch towards Salisbury. On that same date, double track was opened between Newton Tony and Amesbury. So great was the volume of traffic that the double track was extended to Bulford 23 May 1909. Amesbury had three spacious platforms to cater for troops and their supplies, while in addition were three long loading docks.

The First World War saw more camps opening, these were served by the Larkhill Military Railway which curved westwards between Amesbury and Bulford. In addition to serving Larkhill and Rollestone, branches ran to Flying Shed Sidings and Fargo Hospital, the latter line terminating at Lake Down Airfield, Druid's Lodge. Further branches ran to the Handley Page aircraft hangars and Stonehenge Airfield. These latter branches closed in 1923.

Soldiers detrain at
Amesbury. They
were hauled by two
engines. Horse
boxes stand in a
siding to the right.
(Author's
collection)

Amesbury, view
towards Newton
Tony circa 1955.
(Author's
collection)

King George V leaves Lark Hill in the contractor's special train.   (Author's collection)

Bulford.   (Author's collection)

The Second World War saw the Amesbury and Bulford line again very busy and on Sunday evenings a through train from Waterloo was provided for servicemen returning from weekend leave. In 1951 the branch line passenger service was reduced to one train daily and this was withdrawn on 30 June 1952, goods traffic following on 4 March 1963.

In 1917 a 4 mile long 60cm gauge line was laid to Porton Camp and from it a highly curvaceous line led to Winterbourne Gunner Camp. December 1918 was the month when the greatest number of passengers was carried, the total being 18,63 in addition to 1,434 tons of freight. Following the Armistice the five steam locomotives were replaced by petrol engines. Passenger services continued till 1937 when they were replaced by Silver Star buses.

West of Salisbury, on 15 October 1915 a line was opened between Dinton and Fovant Camp. 2½ miles in length it had a ruling gradient of 1 in 35 – very steep for a railway, so to guard against runaways, a catch point was provided to derail a wayward train. When seen that it was under control, the points were held over manually and a green flag, or a green light at night, displayed to signal to the driver that he could proceed. The branch enjoyed its heaviest traffic following 1918 when the camp was used as a demobilisation centre, every day 2,000-3,000 men being discharged. The line closed 18 December 1920, was re-opened on 5 March 1921 and finally taken out of use 15 February 1924. In 1937 the Air Ministry constructed a nine mile long narrow gauge system over part of the track bed to serve its ammunition depot of bunkers set in woodland.

At Chilmark quarry just west of Dinton, a siding opened 10 July 1938 to serve a high explosive bomb store in an old quarry which had provided stone

A 0-6-0 at Bulford. The train comprises of an ex-LSWR brake third and a BR Standard corridor coach. (Author's collection)

A narrow gauge passenger train on the Air Ministry line at Dinton, 12 April 1966. It runs on the formation of the former Fovant Military Railway.   (Author)

AMW No 154 at Chilmark Air Ministry sidings 8 April 1964.   (Author)

for Salisbury Cathedral. The Air Ministry also established a narrow gauge line at Chilmark worked by diesel locomotives and these were transferred at various times to and from the line near Dinton. It was a sensitive site and it is believed that atomic warheads were stored there. Both systems closed on 2 November 1994.

Apart from these two narrow gauge systems, in 1944 Baverstock Sidings were laid down on the up side of the station for use by the USA Air Force. After peace was declared, it became an Admiralty store. In 1948-9 over 40 ex-SR locomotives were cut up by contractors in these sidings, some boilers being recycled for use in factories and market gardens. Private owner wagons were also broken up here The GWR's Westbury to Salisbury line had two military branches. The standard gauge Codford Camp line ran from Codford to the camp 2¾ miles distant. It was constructed by Sir John Jackson Ltd and opened in October 1914. At the request of the War Office, the GWR took over the line in May 1918. It closed on 1 January 1923 and the track was lifted the following year.

From Heytesbury a 3½ mile long standard gauge line ran to Sutton Veny Camp. This line was built by Oliver, Ling & Company in 1916-7. It was designed so that ambulance trains could draw up alongside the military hospital wards set up on a mile-long site. The branch was operated by the GWR from May 1918 and the line closed and lifted by 1923. It was worked by ex-Caledonian Railway 4-4-0Ts No 6 and No 10 alternately. They were stabled at the GWR's Westbury depot and if the GWR was short of locomotives, one was used as shed pilot.

9 **Significant Accidents**

The accident at
Thingley Junction
16 January 1907.

ALTHOUGH WILTSHIRE has had a number of serious railway accidents resulting in death and injury, thankfully only one was really catastrophic.

An event occurred on 3 January 1852 which revealed just how stable broad gauge trains were. The time-interval, rather than the block system of working, was in operation and 20 minutes after a goods train left Chippenham, the Up mail followed, the station master considering that the goods was far enough in advance not to caution the Mail's driver. However, fog had caused rails on Dauntsey Bank to become slippery and due to loss of adhesion the goods train slowed considerably. The fog obscured the tail lamps and the Mail crashed into the brake van at 50 mph, Driver Ellis receiving fatal injuries. Owing to the stability of the broad gauge, only a few passengers were hurt. Others even remained asleep during the event and only woke after the Mail had returned

to Chippenham. Quite unaware that they had been to Dauntsey and back, they complained at the lengthy wait at Chippenham!

Thingley Junction was the scene of two accidents. The first occurred on 5 November 1875 when a Paddington to Bristol express appeared under clear signals, but just as it reached the Home signal, it was thrown to red. The express driver reversed his engine, but could not stop in time, so struck a goods train which had over run red signals. A guard was killed and 12 passengers injured. The well-named commercial traveller, Mr Wright, 'opened his samples of wines and spirits and freely distributed them as restoratives for the sufferers'. The subsequent inquest was not without humour. One witness, Thomas Baker, an upholsterer of Queen Street, Bath, said: 'When the train came to a stoppage, I looked out and seeing the carriage before me thrown over, I thought it was time to get out'.

An almost exact replica of the accident occurred on 16 January 1907 when a Westbury to Chippenham passenger train ran through signals and struck the side of a Swindon to Plymouth goods.

What could have been a terrible disaster happened on 16 September 1893. A down express headed by 2-2-2 No 3021 *Wigmore Castle*, entered Box Tunnel at no more than 44mph and, when rather more than half way through, the leading axle broke causing the engine to derail, part of it fouling the other track just as a train was approaching from the other direction. Fortunately the driver of the up train heard someone yell 'Stop' and closed the regulator reducing speed before the two engines struck.

Within a few minutes the Royal United Hospital at Bath was telephoned and beds prepared for a large number of patients, but in the event, only seven were admitted. 250 men were employed to clear the line. The engines were so tightly wedged that two other engines could not extricate them and a further two were sent for.

A curious sight could be seen at Hay Lane, west of Swindon, on 29 January 1940. The severe weather had brought down the block instrument wires between Hay Lane and Wootton Bassett signal boxes and so 20 minute time interval working was introduced.

Due to problems with frozen points at Swindon preventing acceptance there, four trains stood head-to-tail at Hay Lane signal box awaiting clearance. A fifth train, although driven cautiously, did not spot a waved red lamp until it was 20yd away, so crashed into the fourth. The guard of this fifth train ran back along the line to protect it and successfully stopped the sixth train. In turn the guard of the sixth train ran back to protect it from the seventh. There were now seven trains in the 1½ miles west of Hay Lane signal box. The trouble at Swindon resolved, they moved forward one at a time with the requisite block distance between.

On 5 August 1873 two trains on the single broad gauge Westbury to Salisbury line collided head-on at Bemerton Bridge where the A30 crosses the railway west of the city. Rolling stock piled up and the *Somerset & Wilts Journal* reported that 'the air was filled with piteous cries of the wounded and shrieks of terrified passengers'. The accident was caused by an error at Wilton. The passenger train from Bristol due 4.15pm at Salisbury was 36 minutes later. A mixed goods and passenger train was scheduled to leave Salisbury at 4.35pm and Isaacs, station master at Wilton, not wishing to delay the goods, telegraphed Salisbury that he would hold the down passenger train until the mixed train arrived.

In addition to holding the post of station master, Isaacs also held the posts of booking clerk, telegraph clerk and signalman. Miss Callis, maid to Lady Maud Parry, inquired about luggage and he told her it was 'All right'. The guard of the down passenger train heard this remark and believed it to be said to him regarding the departure of his train. Immediately it left, Isaacs tried to telegraph Salisbury to hold the mixed train, but received no response. He threw off his coat and sped after the train going to Salisbury, but all to no avail.

As the two trains approached each other, *Homer,* a 4-4-0ST heading the passenger train and *Gladiator,* a 0-6-0 the goods, one of the guards and a fireman jumped from the train to the embankment. This act saved the guard's life as his van was smashed to matchwood.

Five of the injured were taken to the Salisbury Infirmary in a first class coach sent from Salisbury, while the less injured were taken to local hotels. Passengers in the coach attached to the goods train escaped with 'a good shaking' as the impact of collision was deadened by the intervening wagons. The damage to rolling stock and locomotives was estimated at £4,000. Thomas Harvey, the passenger train driver, was one of the first employed by the GWR and drove the first train through Box Tunnel. William Tucker, passenger guard from Bristol, died when lockjaw set in.

Station master Isaacs pleaded that he had been harassed the previous day, August Bank Holiday Monday, by having to deal with 5,000 to 6,000 extra passengers who had attended a great fete in Wilton Park featuring Blondin, the famous tight rope walker.

In his report to the Board of Trade Colonel Hutchinson said that he believed telegraphing trains should only be done by a regular signalman and frowned on working a single line by telegraph alone. He added that if both, or even one of the trains had been equipped with continuous brakes able to be operated by the driver, the consequences would have been less serious.

The very worst railway disaster in Wiltshire occurred at Salisbury early on 1 July 1906 when the American Boat Line train from Devonport to Waterloo hauled by L12 class 4-4-0 No 421 derailed on the sharp 10 chain curve killing 24 passengers plus Driver Robins and Fireman Gadd. The overturning train struck a milk train on another line killing its guard an also the fireman on an engine beyond the milk train. Although a 30mph limit was imposed on non-stop trains, it was very considerably exceeded by No 421, its speed being well over 60mph.

The cause of the accident has been an enigma. Driver Robins, an experienced, teetotal driver, sounded his whistle on the approach to Salisbury, this

The overturned express engine No 421 being lifted at Salisbury. (Author's collection)

fact indicating that he was alert and knew his whereabouts. It is thought that his irregular shift patterns in the preceding days disrupted his Circadian rhythm and that after sounding the whistle, he suffered a micro-sleep and thus failed to apply the brakes.

10 **An Overview**

WHAT HAVE railways done for Wiltshire? Before the coming of railways life in the county moved at a slow pace – even getting from one side of Wiltshire to the other was impossible in a day except on the very few stage-coach routes. For many, travel was unnecessary because they lived and worked within walking distance of their homes. Agriculture was mostly dairying, the climate favouring meadows, and butter and cheese stayed fresh long enough to travel to market. Oats were important as horse feed for coaching inns. The introduction of railways caused a dramatic change to the lives of some innkeepers and farmers; innkeepers on once busy roads lost their trade, and farmers had to change to growing other crops.

The railway offered a greater variety of employment than had been available in the district before its arrival. To progress through the railway ranks one needed to move, no longer staying in the same house or even in the same native village. Sometimes only a day's notice was given to report to another station.

The coming of the railway led to a greater use of coal for cooking and heating than hitherto, for, until railways, transportation of coal had been expensive and wood was the alternative fuel. With rail transport available a greater variety of building material could also be used, not just local stone or brick, but different materials brought cheaply from a distance such as slates and tiles which rendered thatch out of date.

With cheap transport, a bacon factory need no longer just supply the district, but the whole country; similarly milk, with its very short life, could be sent by rail to urban markets. The railway enabled the cottager's wife to travel to a larger market town where she could receive a better price for her butter, cheese and eggs, more than offsetting the cost of her ticket.

Railways affected diet: no longer did one have to rely on what was grown in one's garden or was grown locally. Food could be transported cheaply from, or to, other parts of the country. Cattle and sheep were sent from Wiltshire and early potatoes and tomatoes brought in, while such things as bananas could be imported and distributed.

Railways enabled people to gain a broader understanding by travel. The Great Exhibition of 1851 could be reached by cheap excursion from Wiltshire and that meant that many people visited the Metropolis who would not otherwise have done so. Quite a few shops and firms paid the fare for their employees.

The Workmen's Early Morning return enabled people to travel cheaply by rail as long as they reached their destination by 8.00am. This time limit was imposed to prevent white collar workers who were better paid and could afford a full price or season ticket, from taking advantage of cheap fares.

Railways played a vital part in the war effort in both World Wars, particularly affecting Wiltshire as they carried troops, ammunition and other supplies to the south coast, the county being particularly used for ammunition storage, mostly in former quarries. The GWR's Swindon works manufactured items such as guns. The RAF had a large number of camps and stations in Wiltshire. When air raids threatened London, children were evacuated to Wiltshire.

How has passenger transport changed between the eighteen-forties and 2009? In the eighteen-forties, as today, not all Wiltshire settlements were served by rail and road transport was necessary for at least part of the journey. By the nineteen-hundreds many settlements were served by rail, a walk up to two miles to a station being thought not unreasonable. In the early part of the twentieth century there was little alternative to rail travel, but today travel from one part of the county to the other is probably more conveniently done by road, unless other factors come into the equation such as crowded roads, parking problems or lack of driving ability. Because of the closure of local stations, short distance rail commuter traffic is less common than formerly, but in 2009 rail travel certainly comes into its own for long distances and a significant proportion of people live in Wiltshire but work in London, travelling by train daily. Rail is more restful for the traveller and better for the environment.

One difference to rail traffic over the last twenty years is that excursion trains have all but disappeared. Another change is that today's trains are of fixed length and inflexible. Until about forty years ago, a sudden influx of traffic would produce one or several extra coaches or even a duplicate train. Today services are run with the minimum number of vehicles to maximise the investment and overcrowding can be a serious complaint. Rail freight has also changed. In 1849 railways were the common carrier and would transport any item from a small parcel to an elephant or tons of coal. Today the railway only deals with bulk items such as cars from Swindon. A freight train is almost a rare sight in 2009, yet in the nineteenth or twentieth century line-side watchers would have seen as many freight as passenger trains.

And what of the future for the railways of Wiltshire? Here the author might by permitted to indulge his personal vision. I would like to see more encouragement to use the train, rather than the car, for longer journeys. Free station parking would help, perhaps not in larger towns where people should be encouraged to use the bus to reach the station, but certainly at more rural stations. I would like to see plenty of space on trains, rather than passengers packed in airline style. Space is limited in a car and space could pull people from the car into the train. Why is it that an old age pensioner can travel free, say from Swindon to Chippenham by bus, yet has to pay to use the more environmentally-friendly train?

I don't anticipate many more stations being re-opened in Wiltshire because each stop delays a train and if a train is slow people will not use it because it might be quicker to go by road, but Corsham station should be re-opened to relieve some of the traffic trying to enter Bath from the east, and a Devizes Parkway, at say, Patney & Chirton could also fill a want.

As for commercial use, I would like to see the loads of long-distance lorries carried by rail, road being used only for collection and local distribution. This would benefit the environment.

A report assembled by eight companies including Virgin, Scottish & Southern Energy and Arup warns that the peak for cheap, easily available oil production is likely to be reached by 2013. After this, high oil prices will be the long term trend. At the time of writing it appears that electrification of the railway from Maidenhead to Bristol (Temple Meads) could be carried out in the not too distant future. A higher oil price is likely to have an effect on railways because rail transport, as it uses oil more efficiently, will be relatively cheaper than road vehicles. Rail vehicles of the future may be constructed of lighter materials to reduce fuel consumption. Rail has the advantage that it produces between five and ten times fewer carbon emissions per tonne than road transport.

Largish urban areas such as Salisbury and Swindon may use tram-trains with single trams converging on a centre and then being formed into a train to reduce line occupancy through the centre and then uncoupled and sent on radiating lines the other side. Running could be along streets, through tunnels, or along redundant or active railways with spare paths. Taking a wider view, such a system could link Westbury, Trowbridge and Bradford on Avon, perhaps even crossing the county boundary into Bath. Another future development might be a really high speed line between London and Bristol passing through Wiltshire.

And what of those railways closed and not brought back into use? A number of them, their formations almost forgotten except for use as unofficial footpaths, are now becoming official paths and cycle ways offering gentle routes through the heart of the countryside and hopefully away from the sound of road transport.

Suggested Further Reading

Anon, *Holt Junction* (Holt Magazine,1966)

Anon, *A Last Look at Holt Junction* (Holt Magazine, 1967)

Barnsley, M, *Midland & South Western Junction Railway* (Wild Swan Publications Vol 2 1991, Vol 3 1995)

Barrett, D, Bridgeman, B, & Bird, D, *A M&SWJR Album* (Redbrick 1981)

Bartholomew, D, *Midland & South Western Junction Railway* (Wild Swan Publications 1982)

Bridgeman, B, & Barnsley, M, *The Midland & South Western Junction Railway* (Chalford 1994)

Butters, N, *Historical Transport Map of Wiltshire* (Transmap 1993)

Catterell, J, & Falconer K, *Swindon: The Legacy of a Railway Town* (HMSO 1995)

Cooke, R A, *Track Layout Diagrams of the Great Western Railway and BR Western Region* Section 20 *(1988)*, 21 *(1988)*, 23 *(1986)* (Author)

Fenton, M, *The Malmesbury Branch* (Oakwood Press 1977)

Fenton, M, *The Malmesbury Branch* (Wild Swan Publications 1990)

Harper, D, *Wilts & Somerset: A Railway Landscape* (Millstream Books 1987)

Leleux, S A, *Brotherhoods, Engineers* (David & Charles 1965)

Luegg, L H, *The Salisbury & Yeovil Railway* (David & Charles Reprint 1960)

Maggs C G, *The Midland & South Western Junction Railway* (David & Charles 1967)

Maggs, C G, *Railways of the Cotswolds* (Peter Nicholson 1981)

Maggs, C G, *Rail Centres: Swindon* (Ian Allan 1983)

Maggs, C G, *The Calne Branch* (Wild Swan Publications 1990)

Maggs, C G, *The Swindon to Gloucester Line* (Alan Sutton 1991)

Maggs, C G, *Branch Lines of Wiltshire* (Alan Sutton 1992)

Maggs, C G, *Colin Maggs' West of England* (Sutton Publishing 1998)

Maggs, C G, *The Swindon to Bath Line* (Sutton Publishing 2003)

Mattingly, N, & Slater, G, *Bradford's Railway* (Bradford on Avon Preservation Trust 2007)

Mitchell,V, & Smith, K, (All published by Middleton Press):
   Basingstoke to Salisbury (1991)
   Branch Lines of West Wiltshire (2003)
   Fareham to Salisbury (1989)
   Salisbury to Westbury (1994)
   Swindon to Gloucester (2005)
   Swindon to Newport (2004)
   Westbury to Bath (1995)

Nicholas, J, & Reeve, G, *Main Line to the West* (Irwell Press Part 1 2004, Part 2 2007)

Oakley, M, *Wiltshire Railway Stations* (Dovecote Press 2004)

Peck, A S, *The Great Western at Swindon Works* (OPC 1983)

Phillips, D, & Pryer, G, *The Salisbury to Exeter Line* (OPC 1997)

Phillips, D, *From Salisbury to Exeter: The Branch Lines* (OPC 2000)

Priddle, R, & Hyde, D, *GWR To Devizes* (Millstream Books 1996)

Pryer, G A, & Paul, A V, *Track Layout Diagrams of the Southern Railway & BR SR* (R.A. Cooke Section 3 1981, Section 5 1982)

Robertson, K, & Abbott, D, *GWR: The Badminton Line* (Alan Sutton 1988)

Sands, T B, *The Midland & South Western Junction Railway* (Oakwood Press 1959)

Smith,T M, & Heathcliffe, G S, *The Highworth Branch* (Wild Swan Publications 1979)

Thomas, D St J, *A Regional History of Railways Volume 1* (David & Charles 1981)

Tomkins R, & Sheldon, P, *Swindon & The GWR* (Alan Sutton & Redbrick 1991)

Williams, R H, *The London & South Western Railway* (David & Charles Volume 1 1968, Volume 2 1973)